M000226716

From A Small
Naval Observatory

From A Small Naval Observatory

Walter "R" Thomas

Captain, U. S. Navy

Naval Institute Press

Annapolis, Maryland

The assertions and opinions herein are the private
ones of the author and are not to be construed as official
or reflecting on the views of the Department of Defense,
the Department of the Navy, or the naval service at large.

Walter "R" Thomas

Copyright © 1972
by the United States Naval Institute
Annapolis, Maryland

All rights reserved. No part of this book
may be reproduced without written permission from
the publisher.
Library of Congress Catalog Card Number: 72-85341
ISBN: 0-87021-197-8

Printed in the United States of America

To the U. S. Navy's Flying Midshipmen
1946-1950

For two decades my friends have struck
At Hanoi and Toko-Ri;
And their modest part in this Navy art
Deserves a modest plea!

The U. S. Naval Institute will welcome
your comments—pro and con—about this book.
Write to: U. S. Naval Institute *Proceedings,*
Comment and Discussion Department,
Annapolis, Maryland 21402

Preface

This collection of observations is presented as a personal anthology, and the individual chapters are unconnected—or at least remote—from any concept of grand design.

The thoughts expressed in the following articles not only do not reflect the opinions of the Department of Defense or the Department of the Navy but often, in part, are in mild opposition to them. My military colleagues will be among the first to point this out to anyone who has a desire to listen. Yet the solicitation of subsequent military effort is one of the primary reasons that these chapters were written, for there is a need to encourage knowledgeable service personnel to contend publicly against programs and systems (and books) which they believe are inaccurate.

The past reluctance of active duty officers to accept this challenge arises because of the ever present conviction within the military establishment that promotion stops with publication. I hope that more of my capable colleagues will attempt to disprove this theorem and start to express themselves in writing more formidably, for their keen insight for constructive change is useless as an unexpressed insight. Former Vice President Humphrey stated, "America is a free market for people who have something to say and need not fear to say it." The military, as far as I can determine, was not exempted.

Extreme care has been taken to avoid touching on classified material. This has eliminated from public discussion many choice items which must always be left to those civilian writers who normally have the least information on which to base their articles. But it is in these areas that future "in-house" military suggestions should be welcomed and encouraged by senior military and civilian leaders; it is also in these areas that originality is a short stock commodity.

Perhaps a more accurate analysis of each point mentioned in this book will be forthcoming by more ardent advocates. In this respect, I believe Dean Acheson's advice, "How vulnerable are those who explain," will haunt my small naval observatory for a long, long time.

There are many comments which may lead the sensitive to conclude that the author has consumed too many sour grapes. It is therefore most important for the reader to realize that the author has received every consideration in his Navy career, and these tender chapters have been carefully and purposely written—and revised—in a framework of objectivity. I am certain that many who are closely and personally involved with the functions discussed will deny this. I am equally sure that they would have objected no matter how the subjects were analysed.

Finally, there is no wrath intended in this book, for I have encountered none within the Navy. Few of my civilian friends have had such good fortune in their professions. The barbed humor (if it can be found) is not aimed at the jugular vein. Disagreement is anticipated! For this purpose, my colleagues' attention is invited to Job 21:3.

W. R. T.

Contents

If you are to be called upon to face danger and death in the defense of your country, you are entitled to a voice in the shaping of its programs.

United States Representative
Robert L. F. Sikes
Naval War College Graduation Address
14 June 1967

Introduction

Reflections in Water

World War II was a mighty war, a classic war, a nationally accepted war and—in terms of military and moral dogma—a relatively pure, clean, uncluttered, patriotic, and dedicated war. The Atlantic and Pacific mariners who were fortunate enough to survive those massive ocean operations from 1941 through 1945 were rewarded, most appropriately, with medals, promotions, commands, and eventual control of the United States Navy.* This is as it should be.

Since that time, however, there have been a few minor skirmishes involving the fates of the "brothers younger"—the men who entered the Navy after World War II and who have tried diligently to emulate the reputations of their seniors. While concerned primarily with this post-World War II group, the author in no way means to detract from the prestige of the gallant members of a generation before him who gained their glory in a more difficult hour.

But it has been a quarter of a century since World War II ended and during this period the entire personnel structure of the operating Navy has changed drastically, while the administrative structure, in many respects, has stagnated. Today most officers of the rank of captain or below, and almost all of the enlisted men, are too young to have participated in those actions where the Navy's current admirals wrote their reams of history.

This means, for example, that these experienced officers, commissioned between 1946 and 1952, have spent (in relation to most of their seniors) a longer period of time in each junior officer rank. This process has permitted them, while relatively young, to become better acquainted with both Department of Defense policies and the modern Navy's detailed organization. They also are more aware of the technical progress, personnel quandaries, and problem areas—at least at the operational level—than were their

* Hereafter, when the Navy is mentioned, the United States Navy is meant, unless otherwise stated.

World War II predecessors. As division officers for the past two decades, they have studied, often too initimately, the relative poverty of their enlisted men's families, the inability of some seniors to adapt to change, the inherent errors of administrative enterprises which perpetuate themselves, the lack of consideration or coordination which exists in mentally blighted areas of the Navy's shore establishment, and the heart-rending pace of many Washington military leaders who, hamster-like, continue to keep their cages whirling without realizing that they have been disconnected from the operational generator.

This book is but a review of these problems, prospects, hopes, and despairs within the Navy and the nation as some of us think we see them after twenty-five years of fond professional association. It also contains the basic thoughts many young officers have expressed with and without effect for a very long time. This is because original programs have to be forwarded "via" so many subordinate commanders that they are smothered by "obstacle-tricians" before they bear fruit. Many of the military recommendations written by my generation, unhappily, have been consigned to the Kingdom of Via—a military limbo which exists somewhere between the frontiers of the *originator* and the eventual *approving officer*.

Thriving somewhere in the Kingdom of Via are many of the visionary ideas that the Navy is trying to uncover. This book does not pretend to contain any of them; it merely states the opinions of one officer who feels that routing advice along the public highway often is preferrable to directing it toward that isolated Kingdom.

It is, then, only to relate the attitudes, difficulties, and professional positions of the younger officers and men that this book is written; and it is to those who have been the quiet, exemplary, and conscientious leaders of the operating forces at the junior and senior officer levels for the past quarter century that this book is dedicated.

From A Small
Naval Observatory

Systems Analysis Is the Name of the Game But No Two Play It Quite the Same

You are a very kind man, and I think you might be a good king. But if you were to try all your life, you would never be a good gooseherd.

King Maximilian and the Gooseboy

Years ago, when the Navy's directives were considerately "designed by geniuses for execution by idiots," no one really had to worry about very much except the annual court-martialing of ensigns who lost classified material.

For example, it was, as events coursed, more or less accepted that (*1*) supply officers would stock too many of the wrong items and none of the required ones; (*2*) navigators would lose at least one set of binoculars per quarter; (*3*) a few ships would quietly run aground each year and thus deprive Navy captains of their opportunity to sport admiral's stars on their collars; (*4*) friends would get orders to Washington, and an appropriate wake would be held; (*5*) operating accounts would be about half right half the time; (*6*) aircraft squadrons would send pilots out to orbit lighthouses during the last week in June to burn up aviation fuel appropriations and thus make the fiscal year's budget come out even; (*7*) the anticipated percentage of WAVES would become pregnant; and (*8*) records of investigation would clear aircraft carrier officers of liability for pumping sea water into helicopters. It was, all in all, a well ordered and predictable world.

Into this quiet pool of Navy life, disturbed only by wars and

1

reserve officers, splashed an organization known as the Department of Defense (DOD). Short of outright secession from this organization, the Navy, and other services, were not quite sure how to cope with it. It did not occur to many that the Defense Department was not necessarily an antagonist. And, to be completely fair, some members of the Defense Department, after a few years of being sparred and tethered, began to display a certain amount of reciprocal annoyance.

This led, in part, to many, many Defense Department offices which the Secretary of Defense felt were necessary to produce an effectively managed organization that would at least let him know what was going on—especially since the services were not volunteering that information. Whether all of these DOD sub-units were necessary was, and is, a matter of intense debate; but something was needed. Just because the military services were non-profit organizations, there was really no need for them to pursue bankruptcy with such annual enthusiasm. Out of the milieu, eventually, came the "whiz kids," Mr. (Cousin Charley) Hitch's wonderful budget making machine, Dr. Brown's weapons concepts, Dr. Enthoven's systems analysis programs, and the Great Study Age—a period second only to the Great Ice Age in Potomac annals.

It really took the Defense Department two decades to find the control switches, but once they were located, the Good Ship DOD proceeded with full sails. How much it is tacking versus how far it is progressing on its base course is a grainy subject which ferments at many a suburban basement bar in the Washington area, but there is no longer any doubt about the Defense Department's movement.

Although much of the military cooperation with the Defense Department was belated, by 1966 almost everyone had the picture. The Secretary of Defense (Uncle Bob in "E" Ring) had pulled too many clever rabbits out of his Pentagon hat for the services to ignore his fine stage presence. The management magic of systems analysis has thus been accepted, occasionally with enthusiasm, by segments of the military community who have had past reservations about civilian directed operations. Specific programs, however, are often modified by the services at the field level to accomodate internal chaos—and daily at the Washington level to emphasize the difference of opinions on force structures.

The Great Study (and Analysis) Age, unfortunately, tended to build a glacial advance of personnel support requirements out of

2

proportion to the military services' (and even the Defense Department's) ability to contain it. Ironically enough, one of the major organizations needed today, requiring even more people, is an agency to control all of these study and analysis staffs.

Affiliated branches of the government that support or utilize military programs, together with senior service colleges, ad hoc committees, associated universities, civilian contractors, groups within the Joint Chiefs of Staff, esoteric military sections under the control of each service chief, pick-up teams on the staffs of unified and specified commanders, designated analysis centers, and Dr. Enthoven's "denizens of the citadel" are only some of the groups now conducting studies. Some are coordinated, some contradictory, some classified, some public, some jealously guarded, some irrelevant, some needed, some spasmodic, some merely academic, and some as unrelated to tomorrow's world as crystal sets and silent movies.

However they are not, among other things, directed or controlled by a central administrative agency or conducted in a well-planned manner. In fact, we may yet see a "Systems Analysis Study on How to Organize, Coordinate, and Conduct Studies." It may be, within the DOD briar patch, the most valued rabbit of all.

The Aluminum Overcast
and Other Fairy Tales

*And the ship sailed off through the sky, taking
the Lost Boys home to Never Never Land,
where they still live today.*

Peter Pan

During the Berlin Blockade, later in Korea, and most recently in South Vietnam, America's ocean transport specialists
proved that they could supply anything that was needed anywhere
and at anytime. This has impressed the world's Red rascals because no other nations, especially the Communist ones, can ap-
proach the logistical heights of the United States. The flood of
technical, mobile, and flexible base support which Americans can
pour across the seas in an emergency inundates the dry, logistical
minds of even our most critical adversaries.

The success of these efforts, however, has resulted not from
air freight, but from command of the seas. Since World War II the
United States has consistently held this command. Therefore, a
nation which borders on an ocean simply cannot be conquered by
its neighbors if it is under the unlimited protection of the United
States. The question then is not whether America can prevail, but
how it will travail. Since the world is a natural beach resort, how
many of the one hundred ocean-flanking nations is the United
States willing to press to its bosom—and why—and when?

The old British priority system, with all its faults, was a
practical application of balancing a nation's resources against its
world commitments. At the very least it was a planned muddle. It
also was, noticeably, based on sea power. America, however, has
avoided any such categorical considerations of priority areas
abroad. After World War II we did, in a moment of mental lapse,
draw one Asian goal line through the Formosa Strait and (as Sam

4

Goldwyn might note) we included Korea *out*. That cartographical error in foreign policy was rectified by a noteworthy police action.

But America also has been involved in Lebanon, Congo, South Vietnam, Berlin, Cambodia, Laos, Thailand, the Dominican Republic, and Cuban environs. There is little doubt that we could assist Iran, India, Colombia, Formosa, Saudi Arabia, West Germany, Italy, Turkey, Upper Volta, Japan, Iceland, or practically anyone else enveloped in a Red tide. Will we? Who knows? Can we? Certainly! But by air? We don't think so, do we?

Incidentally, it is hard to assess accurately how deeply we have "drawn down" on our experienced sea and air power in both the regular and reserve military forces for each international effort since World War II. Of course, we know how much those operations have cost, how many men were committed, what equipment was furnished, and where the military establishment was thinned to provide the required forces; but we do not know how many men have later left the regular and reserve services specifically because of these contingencies, whether other nations have tergiversated communism solely due to our stand, which domestic programs subsequently have been too sharply curtailed for America's own good, or how many of these world efforts we could support simultaneously in the future. These are the judgment issues which leaders must analyze more thoroughly, preferably before Americans become disenchanted with *all* other nations. As with the tomcat making love to the polecat, our fun in international affairs frankly may reach a point where we have enjoyed about as much of this as we can stand.

Of course, from an experienced viewpoint, this nation still has enough dedicated airmen with technical and administrative skill, in and out of uniform, to do almost anything it wants to. But this factor alone almost spoils us into believing that there is no limit to the sainted works that aviators can accomplish on a moment's notice. They are sort of an international Santa Claus, ready to hop into a spangled sleigh and tinkle about the world doing an evening's good at the speed of light. However, one of these days they may break a leg sliding down a chimney cluttered with opposing forces.

Thus people tend to discount the important fact that our military involvements abroad for the past twenty-five years have succeeded only because America controlled the seas. And our ships traveled unchallenged under a friendly umbrella in that eerie logistical combat support environment where there was no sea and

5

relatively little air opposition. This is mentioned only to point out the fact that the smooth flow of supplies which supported the Berlin Airlift, the Korean Conflict, the Lebanon Landing, and the Vietnamese Commitment often is considered normal by some military planners—and has intrigued others into believing they are working in the real world.

Significantly, most of the uncontested material that supports military endeavors overseas is transported by ships. It always has been! This basic premise has been advertised, without exceptional success, by the Navy. It seems that the very fact that America projects abroad by sea—or it doesn't project at all—is as hard for some people to swallow as gruel pudding.

Any substantial opposition, anytime or anywhere, to America's ocean transportation network would require defensive and logistic supply forces at sea far beyond the Navy's or the nation's current commitments or immediate capabilities. The alternative would be to either mobilize nationally or to disengage in any area outside of the Western Hemisphere.

Some people, of course, realize that over ninety per cent of the supplies sent to support Berlin, Korea, Lebanon, and Vietnam traveled by ship. And it has been obvious that these thousands of ship movements were unopposed. What isn't obvious is the number of forces which would have been required to protect this shipping under more hostile circumstances. This is where some air freight advocates, undeterred by facts, unfettered by statistics, and unhinged by devotion, clamor for a sky full of super sized air carriers which will red ball required supplies to the world's villages in the most colossal demonstration of mass movement since the Great Worcester Salt Train.

The miserable bureaucratic truth is that the underdeveloped nations of the world have, perniciously, a monopoly on underdevelopment—including underdeveloped airfields, oil storage depots, ground handling equipment, repair facilities, ad infinitum. Our U. S. transport planes can get you there—but you will starve to death. In addition, the new superplanes have an unquenchable superthirst. They habitually need tons of fuel to leave the area where they have deposited tons of cargo. And, unlike our giant World War II adversaries, the underdeveloped nations have no Bremerhavens or Yokosukas to capture and exploit where we can later back up our air power at well-developed overseas shipping ports. This Alice-in-Wonderland cycle of aviation fuel requirements and ground support equipment versus air cargo capacity must be em-

6

phasized again and again until the air freight devotees acknowledge that the interests of the nation require a new marine ocean shipping construction program. This is the priority project if the United States is to ever again meet a major commitment abroad. Any alternate program which advocates primary reliance on airborne supply at the expense of ocean shipping would only apply in a short skirmish—such as the Whiskey Rebellion.

And Another Thing I'll Say After I Retire

I wish we could hear the good abbot's bell.

The Inchcape Rock

Military officers normally have weepy pens. It is part of the equipment issued to them when they are first commissioned so they can contradict arguments of (*1*) senior officers when caught in irrational acts; (*2*) foreign merchants, when dunned; (*3*) civilian officials, when issued trivial directives; (*4*) wives, when at sea; (*5*) foreign policy analysts, when writing notes to editors; or (*6*) congressmen, who want their constituents transferred.

This graceful art eventually results in the acerbetic flood of timeless prose which *retired* flag officers release as a long damned torrent of abuse after they leave the service. It is then, and only then, that they unveil their "What's Wrong with the Army/Navy/Air Force/Marines/Coast Guard" epics—the "Why We Failed at (in) the African/Italian/Mexican/Korean/Boxer Campaign" stories—and today, of course, those new dramas titled "How the President/Defense Department/Military/Republicans/Democrats/Communists/Allies Caused Us to Lose the War/Peace/Economic Leadership in Kashmir/Vietnam/Outer Space/Antarctica."

There are, admittedly, tedious and trivial administrative obstacles which discourage these officers from writing controversial articles while they are on active duty; but these deterrents are not meant to be repressive. It is, therefore, surprising to note that the sarcastically constructive suggestions which many retired general officers subsequently reveal to their former colleagues and civilian leaders were singularly lacking when they were on active duty. For some reason their literary minds only started to function after their braid was removed.

Too many *active* duty military men today who inwardly disagree with United States policy in Europe are using old cliches in their printed statements and speeches to back arguments they

8

don't really believe; for example, they maintain publicly that NATO, prepositioning (forward location of arms and equipment), manpower allocations, redistribution (courtesy of former President DeGaulle), and military assistance policies can remain as effective and inflexible as they were from 1950 to 1970 in spite of Europe's new posture. This is a professional exercise in reidentifying justification—a field fast becoming a military specialty. What is needed is a search for rediscovering candor.

New articles contradicting today's programs will be written eventually (after retirement) by many of the senior officers now involved in NATO and other overseas projects. They will be entitled, "What We Could Have Done in Europe (or elsewhere)." But to be of some value they should be written now when they will benefit the nation's leaders rather than after the events. Too often those military exponents of change have had an active part in preventing it.

Perhaps a major reason for this literary caution is the loyal conviction of active duty officers that they should not be critical. Also, it may be difficult for many civilian leaders to accept the idea that the active military man has a stake in United States foreign policies and that his recommendations should be encouraged. Additionally, proof that the suppressive attitude does predominate is quite clear, say the active duty officers, because current directives figuratively require them to keep their pens sheathed, their mouths shut, and their shoes shined. Promotion, according to fable, comes to those who do not ever ripple the executive or legislative waters with foreign policy statements or contradictory budgetary, armament, or construction arguments. In fact, many active duty officers maintain that sound suggestions in these fields are particular anathemas at lower administrative levels because even the soundest logic antagonizes entrenched bureaucracy if it advocates change.

This is not a recent dilemma, for it is a vain search to locate military articles written by active duty officers in the 1930s which argued against neutralism and isolation. Everyone was for "Fortress America." Yet, after World War II, many retired senior military men wrote about the dangers of isolation—which they imply they recognized a decade before Munich. This ex post facto awareness certainly neither consoled nor counseled President Roosevelt when he needed support in 1936 and 1937. It is doubtful that future late bulletins will assist today's leaders.

9

Legislatively retired career officers who repose in their hedged cottages are usually not as vehement as their colleagues who resigned from the service in anger after thirty or more years because of a disagreement or an imagined slight. These officers give vent to a lifetime of frustrations in one huge harangue (available in paperback) about the decades of idiocy they have encountered.

Careful analysis of published works by those piqued patriots does not reveal that they wrote books, articles, theses, briefs, memoranda, or even notes during their active careers which would have brought their inspired ideas and valued vision to the attention of their senior military and civilian leaders. Nor did they stay in their service and fight for improvement.

They disagreed with policy, but avoided involvement. They knew of unsound decisions, but remained silent. They had operational experience, but never bothered to quantify it. They saw error and savored the memory instead of correcting the cause. Most of all, they abandoned their colleagues and then complained about them.

Usually the positive contributions have been made by those flag officers who remained on active duty and fought for improvement, often losing, while their retired contemporaries were publicly tilting against them from a safe literary distance.

Unfortunately, most active duty flag officers have avoided public discussion of any subject except in the professional area where they are, at the time, militarily assigned. Their position, even then, is more often one of classified and private in-fighting rather than published disagreement. While extremely valuable, these tactics still leave the public unaware of the existing internal dissent. Americans are thus left with the impression that their active military leaders always defend executive department or congressional policies. This is not true. The military defends the nation. Elections defend or oppose policy. Of course there is the favorite cliche, always quoted to maverick colonels and commanders, that, "complacency is not the hallmark of flag officers—but that's the best way to become one." When something is grossly wrong, or when it could be better, the military officer should bring it to someone's attention. He normally tells his wife, but she has minimum time to devote to reorganizing the military establishment, bi-lateral treaty structures, or Great Wall pacts. (She might note that some call for more magic than mortar, but her philosophy is incidental.)

What the military services need are fewer officers who drift heaven-ward in the promotion cycle and more who are willing to tote ballast. There are many areas where improvement is needed within the services and in our national and international policies. Active duty military officers can offer sound proposals in these fields, because they are intimately and intentionally involved in them for twenty to forty years. If their proposed ideas are unsound, they have a wealth of senior talent to correct them. The inhibition of limited promotion opportunity or an immediate senior's disapproval should, therefore, deter only the lizard-livered.

Anyone For Tunis?

I have found you an argument; I am not obliged to find you an understanding.

Samuel Johnson

The United States military services have the best organized and most complex war game simulators in the world. These electronic displays can pit known or potential enemy forces against current or future American units in any land, sea, or air environment.

Of course, a few mean remarks about game rules occasionally have been made by sore losers. It seems that war game umpires favor home team victories; and there are the ever present rumors (false) that Parker Brothers and Mattel Toys are really the brains behind the armed forces. The unkindest cut, however, usually comes from those military wives who greet their husbands' return from a hard day's war game by mumbling clever nonsense about grown men playing cowboys and indians.

In spite of these snide remarks, war games have been programmed for hundreds of years, and the appearance of Kamikaze pilots was probably the only event which the Navy had not war-gamed against the Japanese forces prior to World War II. One of the major obstacles in today's war games (as with programming the Japanese suicidal mentality) is that a planned format often stifles originality. War game umpires are reluctant to accept novel tactics which are not considered in the written plot. A typical comment might begin, 'I don't see how we can use that offense without shredding our planned parameters." (Note that war game umpires also talk funny.)

Another war game weakness is that the enemy's brains are often credited as being less devilish than the dynamic minds of American commanders. This can lead to a confrontation between the friendly forces who have programmed modern technology against primitive enemies. Like Little Orphan Annie, war game

12

enemies stumble about naively, peering through blank eyes and mumbling expressionless phrases like, "Gee whillikers, Sandy, we're sinking"—while paddling gamely through the alligators.

This situation arises because the programming groups often brain storm their scenario with an ear that is finely tuned toward the expected results; that is, good guys always win—or at least they don't ever lose. It is not that war game planners are non-objective about an enemy's flexibility, but that they are not *too* objective. The simulated enemy, therefore, who is initially issued a lot of force food during the preview, often is not provided with enough cerebral popcorn to last through the first feature. His stereotyped tactics of 1970, in the minds of many, remain stagnant through 1990; and his technological progress, though fairly planned, still leaves him so unaware and unresponsive to a deteriorating situation that he seldom can row his way out of Green Scummy Creek.

Navy intelligence officers, who are always accompanied by a small briefcase and a large watch, usually provide the war game information on potential enemy forces. Their data are remarkably accurate, but these oracles of the salt set are often mugwumps when asked for their projected opinions. Their rationale usually meanders within such statements as, "though Old Blue will have 17 of these by 1980, we have no hard information that the Old Blue commanders can have their forces trained in using Fragettes in a combat environment. In addition, half of their Fragettes are made of glutsum alloy and we don't know if glutsum can withstand a sustained firing rate of 120 kitsocks a minute." Having once wound their instrument, intelligence officers then allow the Navy planners to turn it on. Sometimes it plays music, but mostly it grinds hash.

Once a war game commences, it is in the hands of operational experts. The word "expert," as used by the Navy, often means someone from out of town; occasionally it means a civilian with a foreign accent, but these personages are usually more expensively labled "consultants." (Incidentally, any budding genius should take a course in foreign accents rather than foreign languages. Exorbitant consultant fees are now paid by our government to those who have a command of broken English.) The Navy war game expert usually is a specialist from a cruiser, submarine, aviation squadron, supply depot, or other field activity who is senior enough to understand what intelligence officers haven't said. He can also form a quite capable combatant force equal to the vagaries of what will soon be designated in a written plan as "the

13

situation." He is usually chosen because he is old enough to have absorbed most of the historical errors which his young assistants try to reincarnate as novel ideas guaranteed to win wars.

As the game develops both friend and foe lose forces, scream for unavailable replacements, try to form their players into lynch mobs against the umpires and, generally, gather a high measure of bloody enthusiasm. Even personal greetings can slip into secret war game reports, such as a mock casualty message or an irrelevant teletype dispatch stating, "May your mother-in-law live forever." The umpire's idea of the war game, of course (when he is not chasing down facetious message writers), is to keep the game going—that is, never let either side move "into check" or gain control of *both* Park Place and Boardwalk.

Lifelong enmities have reportedly evolved from these mock wars. Professional gamesmen, however, believe that the process at least evaluates stupidity early in an officer's career pattern and thus results in personnel procurement economies. And the weapon's evaluators claim that it is the only logical way to prove to the cost-effectiveness DOD convent in Washington that there is a dire need for an anti-Fragette weapon in next year's budget. In any event, war games have taken their impregnable position in military planning techniques and operational weapons' evaluations. Perhaps, as with the jousting tourney, mortal combat may again consist of only two participants. In the future they might face each other across a mammoth electronic display with the fastest step relay commander declared the winner. At least it would allow the ladies, once again, to be on hand with favors for the men.

But, Sir!
This *Secret* Textbook
Clearly States . . .

Men who spar with Government need, to back their blows, something more than ordinary journalistic prose.

Rudyard Kipling

At the risk of alienating my colleagues in other military services, I would like to opine that the Navy manual which describes the military planning process is the best coordinated and best written document (for carrying out a combat mission) that has ever been devised. This is because it was composed primarily by veteran personnel—with only a minimum input by administrative (Pentagon) helpers who tried to smooth over what they imagined to be the rough spots in creative writing. Conversely, the joint-service planning manuals seem to have been conceived largely by administrative specialists, and experience seems to have had only an incidental part in their constructive efforts. Anyone who has used both processes to plan a campaign has either noticed this discrepancy or has programmed his operational forces from a source of ignorance.

The Navy manual has evolved from the honest errors of those who participated in unguided miscalculations, such as Tarawa. It also recognizes that the enemy is equally subject to such a lapse of memory as the strategic failure of the Japanese to follow up the initial tactical success at Savo Island. All the Navy does, in essence, is to point out to the military commander that if he follows a planned thought process he will not overlook the essential points which have been subject to oversight in the enthusiastic environs of past battles. Unlike the joint service guidance, the

15

Navy process is unconcerned with such post-conflict considerations as the reconstruction of local health and sanitation facilities, believing that the weight of these problems is hardly necessary when facing a massive and capable attacking force. The problem, as nautically depicted, consists of beating the enemy. The answer, as other manuals see it, is to assume that he has been beaten. These latter-day, rose-colored guides merely concentrate on what to do with him after he is defeated. Although the joint service formats are most optimistic, the Navy directives seem to indicate that the primary purpose of an attacking military force (which is victory) should be given, coincidentally, primary consideration.

The ornate joint planning processes, of course, are often just the residue of literary boredom. As a result, clear-cut pathways are strewn with administrative brush. For example, one can assign an option to each picayune campaign consideration, but the fact that high tide occurs at dawn can only be viewed in so many ways. A pedantic affection for discussing the esthetic value of tides to native worshipers, the possibility of a tsunami, the local economics of fisheries, or the furnishing of a cod god to replace the one destroyed by the invading force are wonderful asides to the task at hand, but hardly pertinent to victory.

The only way to describe the Navy process and the beauty of its simplicity, once understood, is to describe its five step *format* in purposely unclassified terms.

Civil War Operations Order #1123

Situation: Gentlemen, the Yankees hold that ridge.

Mission: We're going to move them off.

Concept of Operations: Wilkens, you hit them on the right. Mc-Gruder, you charge them through the middle. Tuttle, you flank them from the left.

Logistics: We'll eat when we're finished.

Coordination and Control: I'm going up on this hill and watch!

Unfortunately, there is no way to describe the joint service process in unclassified terms, nor really any need to attempt the project. It does strive valiantly to predict every possibility but, as a result, may mislead a commander into believing he is coping with a situation which *must exist*—because the problem was *planned for.*

This joint planning process is constantly subject to revision. Perhaps, and hopefully, the relative simplicity of pre-victory strat-

16

egy, tactics, communications, intelligence, and logistics may receive priority consideration in future Washington tomes.

Of course, all Navy manuals are not perfect—nor always accurate. It takes considerable time to update information, approve doctrine, issue changes, and distribute revised tactics on a Navy-wide basis. Because of this time lapse, inexperienced personnel often mistakenly accept the data in the available classified publications as gospel, even though some of it has been outdated for years. Incidentally, if a few of these more ancient classics were to fall into enemy hands, it would take them years to fathom our documented ignorance.

It is enlightening (though discouraging) to review the fantastic number of classified operational publications in all military services. In fact, the sheer mass of this material could only be viewed appreciatively by an unemployed librarian. It is doubtful if any one person has ever read all of these esoteric military encyclopedias, and it is certain that a minimum of study has been dedicated to their coordination. Myriad information has been spastically inserted into them for three decades. They have been written by different authors, issued at various times, and substantively revised hardly at all. Since they are generally accurate, however, there is no internal, collective enthusiasm for redrafting these mastodonic manuscripts. The process of screening, editing, revising, coordinating, and publishing the information in all of them in a more brief and logical manner would be comparable to condensing the Bible into a three-page article for *Reader's Digest*.

The classified operational publications of other services are, to be generous, as badly mangled as the Navy's. With the current emphasis on producing more technical fodder than can be digested mentally, it is doubtful that anyone will improve the format of those many overaged publications, though they deserve to be recast in a more manageable mold.

It is more likely that they will be replaced by other documents which contain equally as much incomplete and uncoordinated (but more recent) information. This is death by superimposition, a peculiar type of directed administrative demise favored by literate military men who must justify their staff tours of desk duty by issuing something *new*. Attention to previous manuals is not part of this systematic process for, as everyone knows, credit is given to those who author original publications, not to those who patiently revise the old.

This is really a somewhat sad problem, for a few of these

17

older manuals deserve more than either insouciant neglect or indifferent reverence. Their current use as a casual index or roving reference in operational and academic training environments still provides them with a certain authoritative stature. They really require an imaginative program that would provide for collectively updating and periodically reorganizing these venerated volumes into a composite set of useful and interrelated operational manuals. In the Navy, this project, though tedious, would restore many to their original active duty status as fleet guides. Such a controlled venture also might tend to thin out the stock in the Navy's ever increasing literary menagerie by requiring that classified operational information be placed into a logical frame of *existing* thought before authorizing its release to the fleet preserve. Operational manuals, like expensively bred rabbits, will only become valuable when their output is, once again, subject to unemotional control.

It's the Captain's Turn to Get the Coffee

The great god Ra whose shrine
once covered acres
Is filler now for cross-word puzzle makers.

Keith Preston

Once upon a time there were only a few senior Navy officers in Washington. This was because a rather sound and fundamental system of the ancients decreed that naval officers, with minor exceptions, should be splashing about in the oceans or port waters of the world doing nautical things. It was true that station, school, recruiting, training, and headquarters assignments required bodies, but usually the sluggish sea/shore rotation system, together with an annual flow of problem people, filled all the potholes that old salts, with their briny proclivities, snidely referred to as "damn shore duty billets."

It was common to find warrant officers and chief petty officers who bragged of twenty or more years of shipboard duty, and even senior officers could be pressed into admitting that fourteen or more years of their carrers were spent in sea assignments. Their corroded gold braid was their hallmark, and the sea was their sanctuary. Today it's the Pentagon bus terminal!

After World War II, the permanent military invasion of that five-slabbed architectural wonder (sometimes bitterly referred to as a perpetual monument to inefficiency), together with the amoebic slithering of parkways around Washington and the explosive expansion of the Navy's shore establishment, brought about that inexplicable proportion which Parkinson so accurately evaluated when he described the sad plight of the British Navy between World War I and World War II. (As ships were taken out of commission and as there were fewer and fewer operational units each year, the number of personnel hired to support them increased annually.)

It would not be altogether inaccurate to state that there are now more senior naval officers in Washington and environs wandering about looking for coffee than there are in all of the Navy's ships, submarines and aircraft squadrons; and Washington has only part of the braid parade which is not *operationally* active. The civilian staff supporting this "peopleopolis" is even more impressive. It is only fair to add that the Pentagon Navy is not the only military employer of senior officers, executives, and civilian managers in that concrete carousel.

And what do the thousands of officers do? Are they out improving golf handicaps every afternoon? Puttering about their middle class houses? Chasing secretaries, perhaps? Unfortunately not. Every one of these beached mariners is working about sixty hours a week on as ulcer-ridden a variety of sedentary projects as man has ever invented to irritate his duodenum. Some call it, "busy work."

There are naval officers (other services are equally at fault) involved in desk jobs governing the entire spectrum of international policy, contingent planning, weapons systems, personnel management, public relations, logistics, intelligence, communications, strategy, tactics, foreign (and civil) affairs, international economics, space projects, weather analysis, chart making, and oceanography. Others are also involved in those omnipresent instant research projects which recently have inundated military operations with the greatest flow of goop since the Maryland Marmalade factory exploded.

Generally, this formidable array of nautical coaching talent should have only one object in mind—to improve the equipment and the capabilities of the players who, in this instance, would be the officers and men swinging on the end of the hook in the operating fleets.

Any examination of the immediate influence of the shore establishment on the improvement of fleet operations is, however, somewhat disappointing. The deployed ship, submarine, or aircraft squadron commanding officer does not find, emanating from headquarters, brilliant tactical doctrine, novel ideas of weapon employment, answers to his low re-enlistment or officer retention problems, solutions to his spare parts melange, or even financial solace for the families of his men (who live in a state of marginal poverty and in a quandary of administrative frustrations when the husband is overseas).

What the shore establishment does produce, unfortunately, is an ever increasing burden on the slimly manned operating forces. There is a constantly building pyramid of required operational and maintenance reports, personnel questionnaires, leadership program notes, safety presentations, physical fitness test cards, management directives, special inquiry forms, performance charts, inspection and pre-inspection records and training, and medical and counseling lectures. For example, if an operating aircraft squadron attempted to give every lecture on each subject that is directed by higher authorities (who, incidentally, have never coordinated their requirements) there would seldom be time for either flying or maintenance.

Of course it is not feasible to eliminate the jobs of thousands of senior Navy officers who are working ashore for the Joint Chiefs of Staff, the Chief of Naval Operations, the Chief of Naval Material, the Unified Commanders, and hundreds of other shore-based staffs; but there are many who believe a move in that direction is desirable.

Of course efforts to reorganize navies have been made ever since mariners started smashing their galley oars in boarding drills, and never has such copious data been compiled in reorganization studies—with so little effect—than in the volumes which have restratified the Navy's shore establishment time and again since World War II. These studies and agreements (Key West vintage), to be quite fair, conscientiously were made by sincere and determined men who believed that more would be accomplished than a mere lateral transfer of authority. But, as old seafaring philosophers have wisely noted, "The more staffs change, the more they remain the same—only bigger."

Currently many of the experienced admirals, captains and commanders in this shore establishment are working at a Madison Avenue pace on projects which often could be as easily handled by nautically inexperienced civilian college graduates. Many of their shore jobs are basically unrelated to their initial goal as naval officers—command at sea! More importantly, they often are unrelated to any other naval officer's goal. But shore establishment staffs are headed by officers of exceptionally high rank, as every harried, junior, seaborne commanding officer knows—and there are more desks than ships!

These senior savants, marooned in mass on their mahogany

islands, work endlessly preparing position papers, drafting instructions, writing briefs, orating at conferences, debating at joint service meetings, and researching their assigned "Giant Study" ventures. Often their work duplicates or at least tends to overlap the task underway in some other office, but it may be years before this fact is discovered.

A Giant Study, for example, is usually classified *Sacrosanct* or above, so very few outside people even see it. Those who do see it, if they are from a different staff or military service, tend to disagree with it. Subsequently these cross-service associates will launch their own Study to clarify the first epic. Since each service (and even each service staff) may initiate its own study project, all military services, at any given time, have more information on any subject than they know what the hell to do with.

A Study may be slanted, incomplete, inaccurate, or occasionally correct in every detail; in any case, it usually represents the tedious efforts of many shore-bound senior officers who have dedicated hundreds of hours to the project, as they see it. Of course, few people will ever read it! These officers, incidentally, are not incompetent. It is just that many of them are charged with the same task as an Olympic discus thrower—to do something absolutely worthless more capably than anyone else.

Naturally there is no central casting office for these voluminous studies. An outsider, such as the commanding officer of a Navy ship, has no idea which studies are underway. If he should be so rash as to request a copy of a specific Giant Study, it is doubtful if he could find a military office in Washington which would take the responsibility for sending a copy to him. He has encountered the shore establishment morass.

These senior officers in shore duty billets also have found that twenty-plus years of naval service and experience do not guarantee them immunity from trivia, allow them time to direct their efforts toward a better Navy, or even get them an assigned parking spot in the Pentagon car lot.

On a Clear Day You Can See Tomorrow's Assignment Policy

But an ability to persuade, by whatever means, is largely meaningless unless there are goals toward which the means of persuasion can be directed relevantly and effectively.

H. B. Westerfield

No one without a sense of humor should be assigned to Washington, D. C., for duty. Humor, in the maelstrom of government, really should be as available by prescription as some of the more powerful yet less effective sedatives. Humor can prevent madness. Sedation can only delay it.

Fortunately the Navy's personnel assignment officers all have a sense of humor. Many credit this group phenomenon to the careful selection of the breed. Others claim that these men make so many silly assignments that they just naturally absorb hilarity as an on-the-job fringe benefit. A few dour souls, who have been the miscast recipients of unwanted orders and are less objective about assignment policies, protest that an assignment officer's heart actually is as twisted, hard, and black as a piece of last Halloween's licorice.

Personally, I favor the second of the three theories, for it is difficult to issue as many sets of foolish orders as these gentlemen generate without letting an occasional titter seep into your bloodstream. Once a Japanese-speaking friend of mine was sent to non-

Japanese-speaking Guam because ". . . that's as close to Japan as I could find a spot for you."

Every government worker, civilian or military, has a bag of tales about assignment policies, or the lack of them, in his particular profession. The fact that assignment officers in the armed services usually work ten or more hours each day and have about six times more personnel careers to attend to than they can possibly handle makes each unusual situation more understandable, though not less funny.

Officer and enlisted assignments, of course, could be coded and computerized. This would allow rotation and job relief, on a chronological basis, to be more efficiently handled by specially trained personnel. In fact, if the unmanageable naval officer billet code system had ever been given a good wash, computer assistance could have been accomplished years ago. The spectre of the machine, however, has brought a quiver to the heart of every assignment section in Washington for years. The least mutinous breath which utters the suggestion that personal human warmth does not drip on every set of orders causes the very stars to tremble among the hierarchy. But assignment officers know! Oh, how they know! However, the code of knighthood, being relatively sacred, requires death before divulgence. And efforts at career manglement are at least directed without personal bias.

Of course, a capably quick-witted assignment officer has to immediately respond to a hundred phone calls and personal visits each day. This is a natural hazard which every billet weaver faces bravely, even as he would tangle with a less determined enemy in another environment—such as combat. His challenges originate from officers and enlisted men who want to know where they are going next or, if they already have received their orders, why they are going *there.* Inquiries also splash in from wives, admirals, friends, and other controlling agencies who are fond of informing assignment officers that diaster is about to visit them unless they reconsider the effect of their incompetent placement policies.

Insurance sense dictates that every assignment officer must maintain a ready catalog of standard, unassailable answers which will sooth the savages. This list usually contains about 17 *standard answers,* 93 *special retorts,* and the favorite *all-American cliche.* Even these alert responses do not guarantee an assignment officer's freedom from assault, but if they are always uttered as a soft spoken appeal to reason, they will, hopefully, continue to prevent

24

the disenchanted and the irate from banding together for a mass attack.

As an example, a *standard answer* for an East Coast destroyer request (which has been ignored) might be, "you're going to a West Coast minesweeper because you haven't been on the West Coast before." Experience and logic, of course, can destroy this argument, but assignment officers depend on verbal rapidity to befuddle their colleagues. In addition, the personal touch and correct vocal emphasis is the hallmark of a successful assignment officer. Failure to appreciate this has sent capable and determined men to professional oblivion.

A *special retort* usually begins with a more personal but wildly illogical opening that, because of its very imprecision, somehow seems to make sense. The assignment officer listens patiently and then leaps in with something like this, "you're being sent as officer-in-charge of the Cat Island Bird Sanctuary because you're an aviator." This usually throws anyone under 32 off balance. The *special retort*, however, continues, "we also considered that you haven't had a command before, and the liaison consultant in the Department of Agriculture personally picked you after reviewing the records of 23 of our top flight officers." The assignee is usually banding yellow-billed clap hangers for three months before he realizes that the honor bestowed on him was undeserved.

The *all-American cliche* (too often utilized by the novice, but carefully savored for special circumstances by desk deans) usually begins with the slow pitch, "now I know Admiral Toptech wants you on his Polaris staff and you're a missile school graduate," and ends with a fast breaking curve, "but *we* need an arresting gear officer on the aircraft carrier *Neverhome Island,* and *we* are sending that carrier out to the Mediterranean next month with five jet squadrons on board to support United States foreign policy in Europe. Your outstanding record and the *needs of the service* require that *we* get you out to that ship on a *priority* basis." This appeal to national pride is impregnable. It is not flagrant; the assignment officer does not actually press desk buttons which launch a red, white, and blue rocket, play a tape of "The Star Spangled Banner," or briskly raise a small, fluttering flag. The effect is the same!

In summary, no personnel assignment officer can operate successfully in Washington without an adequate understanding of assignment mythology. It also helps if he believes that the answers are *true,* but this is not as important as the ability to *convince*

25

others *that they are true.* It is sort of a verbal alchemy, whereby base facts are made to appear as golden nuggets of truth.

During my tours of duty in Washington, I knew many assignment officers. The few I liked personally, I never really understood. These individuals, however, were the most professionally successful in their field, for their very aura of friendly unintelligibility was the rare and priceless combination needed. This mystic fog of disarming philosophical ether always distinguished the outstanding personnel assignment officer from the mediocre.

Ode to the Navy's Selection Boards

They cross their Lake by a firefly lamp,
and paddle their white canoe.

Thomas Moore

Selection boards within the Navy are widely regarded as the best in the military services. They are as perfect, or as imperfect, as any system can be which depends on one human being's subjective evaluation of another. The major problems arise when, almost concurrently, different selection boards meet on varied subjects to consider the same people. For example a postgraduate school selection board may choose one individual as an outstanding candidate to attend a senior institution, while a promotion selection board, meeting in the same year, may fail to promote him. This has led to the carousel effect where an officer who has grabbed one brass ring suddenly slips off his bobbing horse. Initial education at the Naval Academy, incidentally, has been known to save one from taking an otherwise dangerous fall.

Of all the selection boards (ship command, aviation command, postgraduate education, promotion, service schools, war colleges, etc.), the promotion boards tend to be the most objective; at least the members seem to expend more effort thrashing their way through the ever present mass of conflicting data. However, it has been argued, with some justice, that much of their time is spent not in seeking direction, but in awaiting divine guidance.

The deliberations of their assembly also have been compared to a wine-tasting contest where, ostensibly, Californian and French judges will rule on the merits of New York State grapes to prevent favoritism. As yet there is no way to avoid having a former New Yorker, or a man married to a New Yorker, or a summer resident of New York on the judging platform.

To be fair, promotion boards have about as much maneuverability as a barracuda in a bathtub. This confinement results not from their lack of experienced, analytical talent, but from the Navy's "fitness report" system. These reports are the annual grading slips, similar to the quarterly school cards issued to children. The reports are not as inane as the immortal kindergarten determinations that "Peter doesn't hop well," or that "Lester fights sandbox hour," but you get the idea.

The wonder is that the Navy's promotion boards today still do as fine a job as they have always done with the inputs provided, for too many sow's ears are still described, in fitness reports, as beautifully fashioned silk satchels. The rating system, ironically, is carefully composed but carelessly used. (Most systems usually are.) In the Navy, officers are graded as either *outstanding, exceptional, superior, excellent, acceptable, marginal,* or *unsatisfactory* in 14 separate categories, such as *initiative, loyalty,* etc. The format is fine, and even the most clumsy assassin could gently terminate an officer's career with such a varied choice of weapons. But this is not the problem. Overrating is the greatest curse.

One must know what the phrases mean at the working level to understand why selection boards have as many difficulties as a titwillow in a typhoon. Friendly natives who speak the mother tongue know that the following wily translations apply.

Outstanding	a stellar officer
Exceptional	not quite stellar
Superior	a bit dull
Excellent	mediocre
Acceptable	unacceptable
Marginal	criminality suspected
Unsatisfactory	criminality proven

The problem, then, is that a commanding officer feels obligated to use the top *two* categories on the majority of his officers and save (or savor) the remaining grades for any incompetent lad who has mistakenly been granted a commission. Since there are few of the latter, a promotion board operating within its legislative promotion limits for a given year may have to sift 400 officers from any group of 1,000—wherein most of the officers have been graded highly as promotional potentials. As dictated by such a precept, 600 unhappy individuals who honestly anticipated an advancement in rank will be culled out and sent to the outer limits of civilian life with nothing but a bag of sour apples. This annual event is also known as "observing the pass-over."

There are additional written areas and blank spaces for extensive personal remarks on the fitness report sheet but, in most instances, the old halo effect (stressed in Sociology I) inhibits the entire fitness report program. A good officer normally receives top grades across the board, regardless of the consideration which is supposed to be given to each category; and, as the officer becomes more senior, he automatically becomes *More Outstanding* (although there is not, as yet, such a column).

If fitness reports were bounced back to every commander who overrated his officers, then some serious soul searching might be done by the now complacent Navy bureaucracy. The argument against such a program is that any "guidance" system would tend to (*1*) dehumanize individuals and (*2*) direct the actions of commanding officers—two of the more absolute taboos. However, the fact that the Navy has eighty per cent of its senior officers in the top ten per cent performance category should bother somebody. And the fact that the promotion board seems to use different and more objective standards than other selection boards should afford some young coordinate mind an opportunity to carve a career niche for himself by standardizing all selection board procedures. God help him, however, if he suggests using a computer.

The military also could return to the reporting system of yesteryear, and it is certain that the selection boards would find their task easier. A glittering example of how they did these things in the old days is this report in the archives, filed 150 years ago by the noted General Lewis Cass.

Lower Seneca Town
15 August 1813

Sir: I forward a list of officers of the 27th Regt. of Infty. arranged agreeable to rank. Annexed thereto you will find all the observations I deem necessary to make.

Respectfully,
I am, Sir
Your obt. Servt.

Lewis Cass

27th Regt. Infantry

Alex Deniston-Lieut. Col., Comdg.	A good natured man.
Clarkson Crolins- First Maj.	A good man, but no officer.
Jesse D. Wadsworth- 2nd Maj.	An excellent officer.
Captain Shotwell	A man of whom all the unit is speaking ill. A knave despised by all.
Captain Thomas Earle	Indifferent, but promises well.
Captain Allen Reynolds	An officer of capacity, but imprudent and a man of violent passions.
1st Lt. Jas. Kerr	Merely good, nothing promising.
1st Lt. William Perrin 1st Lt. Danl. Scott 1st Lt. Jss. I. Ryan	Low vulgar men, with the exception of Perrin. Irish and from the meanest walks of life—possessing nothing of the character of officers and gentlemen.
1st Lt. Robert P. Ross	Willing enough—has much to learn with small capacity.
2nd Lt. Nicholas G. Garmer	A good officer but drinks hard and disgraces the service and himself.
2nd Lt. Steward Elder	An ignorant unoffending Irishman.
2nd Lt. McKonkey	Raised from the ranks—ignorant, vulgar and incompetent.
2nd Lt. James Garrey	A stranger in the regiment.

2nd Lt. Piercey 2nd Lt. Thomas G. Spicey	Raised from the ranks, but behave well and promise to make excellent officers.
2nd Lt. Oliver Vance 2nd Lt. Royal Geer 2nd Lt. Miars 2nd Lt. Crawford 2nd Lt. Clifford	All Irish—promoted from the ranks —low, vulgar men without any one qualification to recommend them— more fit to carry the hod than the epaulette.
Ensign Rehan	The very dregs of the earth. Unfit for anything under heaven. God only knows how the poor thing got an appointment.

Though the current Navy system is imperfect, it is still comparatively rated as the best among the services today—and surely the kindest. For example, one would have to search diligently in modern Navy files for even the slightest slur against the Irish.

Mirror, Mirror
On the Wall,
Who's the Pilot
Best of All?

People don't ask for facts in making up their minds. They would rather have one good, soul-satisfying emotion than a dozen facts.

Robert Keith Leavitt

The Navy's officer promotion program is not only subjectively honest; it is relatively rapid. Naval officers often are selected for promotion to commander about two years earlier than their contemporaries in other services. This has encouraged many outstanding individuals (and, admittedly, others) to choose the Navy as a career, for it is possible to become a Navy commander at age 35.

Naval aviators, however, have become orphaned under this "senior-youth" system. Since squadron leaders are chosen by yet another separate squadron command board from the list of newly promoted commanders, the many commanders who are not *additionally* selected as squadron skippers immediately after their promotion to commander become, in effect, retired aviators on desk duty. The Navy simply does not have operational flying jobs for them. This means that each year more than one-half of the newly promoted aviation commanders who choose to remain in the Navy (for the maximum allowable period of 26 years of commissioned service) will not usually fly in operational squadrons during their last ten years of active duty. Thus the Navy loses, or at least fails to utilize, an effective and experienced flying cadre for a full decade; and this mass hibernation happens every fall.

32

The annual squadron command board is charged with the unpleasant annual assignment of analysing all these factors before they antagonize half of the new aviation commanders in the Navy. It is argued that the board cannot be wholly objective, nor wholly subjective. Some have complained that they are mostly rejective. Others maintain that they have proven to be predeterminative; that is, on their way to their board meeting in Washington, they have had a mystic visitation which, somehow, has fixed certain names in their minds which they could not later deny.

After the squadron command board has folded its Ouija board, the bedeviled assignment officer is tasked with the placement of all those new aviation commanders who were not considered by the squadron board as fair and lovable. Although there are many desk jobs for aviation commanders, the movement of these experienced and senior "non-command" aviators is comparable to the Trek of the Boers. In the first place they are now the dregs of the naval aviation market and, in the second place, they refuse to acknowledge it. One assignment officer, speaking of a similar group years ago, said that his problems could be solved if three hundred aviation commanders would desert. But it was one of those unbearably hot days in Washington, and he certainly didn't mean it.

Those Bureau of Naval Personnel assignment officers, who also have to cater to eternal spring, astronauts, irate wives, Antarctic requirements, and incidental wars, are the fall guys who must console and counsel the many unchosen aviation commanders who descend on them each October after the squadron command board selects and rejects future squadron commanding officers. The harried assignment officers' last entrenched position where they ward off the losers is, "even though an aviator is not selected for squadron command, he may still become a Navy captain." This is not a sound argument, but the record is played—like the crooked village roulette game—because it is the only wheel in town. Of course, at age 35 these new commanders are too old to play with airlines and too young to tend bees. They also know that their future promotion opportunity to the exalted rank of Navy captain—without a squadron command—is as slim as a leprechaun's promise.

Another favorite assignment officer retort is that, "promotion depends on the way you perform in your assigned job, rather than the job itself." This response approaches the status of the Mad Hatter's belief that one should celebrate "unbirthdays" because a greater opportunity for happiness exists. Specifically, most other duties will not advance an aviator to the rank of Navy captain, but command of a squadron probably will.

Another professional obstacle to promotion, of course, is that you can be one of the world's greatest aviators, but if you have not had a well-rounded career pattern which includes, primarily, a tour as a squadron commanding officer (together with assignment to Navy schools, staff duty, Washington bureaus, ships, etc.) your promotion opportunity to Navy captain is meager. On the other hand, you may have become so well-rounded that you are fundamentally spherical and thus have no direction at all. One officer believed that he had been so well planned around that he had been professionally bypassed.

There probably is something wrong with an alternate system of selecting aviators for squadron command after 18 or 19 years of commissioned service and seeing how they perform immediately before they are considered for promotion to captain at age 40 or 41. There also must be a fault in the idea of using captains as commanding officers of patrol, experimental, utility, reconnaissance, and training squadrons and having aviation commanders assigned as subordinates in these squadrons for another four or five years of operational flying. Someone, however, must incline an ear toward the waste which results when so few of the highly paid naval aviators over age 35 are operationally employed.

The civilian airlines may wonder how the Navy's manpower gap has survived in multi-engine aviation with a junior officer system. This is not to say that a majority of other senior Navy officers are really operationally employed in aircraft squadrons, or on ships, or on submarines, but only that in aviation an even greater amount of talent lies dormant—and preferably silent.

34

The Care and Feeding of Flag Officers!

It was Din, Din Din! You 'eathen, where the mischief 'ave you been?

Rudyard Kipling

An admiral's aide once moaned that his entire purpose in life seemed to consist of scheduling cars and locating caramel candies. "Not regular caramels, you idiot! I want the caramels with peanut butter centers."

Assignment as an admiral's aide is, by reputation, a highly prized billet. One reason this persistent fable exists is because an aide will meet, professionally, a more senior group of military leaders who may, on reflection, favorably remember him at some remote date—for instance, when they are screening names for promotion.

Fundamentally it is a prestige position which, at best, permits a carefully selected junior officer to acquaint himself with the mature decisions of capable staff officers, learn the techniques of decision engineering, and gain an immense insight into the plans, programs, and operations which he may someday be called upon to generate by himself.

This myth of happiness among the stars always has been a permanent part of naval lore. An admiral's aide, within the sanctum, is viewed as a white-robed disciple. Perhaps this pleasant vision should remain as fantasy forever, like Santa Claus and the Easter Bunny. No joy comes from the factual knowledge which skulks into men's minds under the name of reality. Unfortunately the only way to retain one's beliefs is to avoid conversations with the experienced. In this case, the theory is shattered by talking with either (*1*) many admirals, or (*2*) any aide. It seems that aides and, to some extent, other staff officers, identify themselves as capable operational people who are slowly being suffocated by trivia. Often

35

they cannot even recall the date on which this mental emphysema was diagnosed as malignant. Assignment as an aide defies all "antidotization," and becomes, too often, a tragic and insidious method of occupational assassination.

Most admirals are between fifty and sixty years old, combat trained in World War II, experienced in surmounting bureaucratic obstacles, familiar with Defense Department detours, knowledgeable of Capitol Hill pressures and peregrinations, intolerant of both youth and administrative error, sensitively aware of the niceties of protocol and seniority, generally ignorant of the individual enlisted man's problems, overzealous in demanding that naval projects should be assigned national economic priority, well educated in a broad academic spectrum, scrupulously honest (therefore, while financially comfortable, comparatively poor), convinced that junior officers are incompetent, and defenders of many Navy systems which are anachronistic (My Navy, right or wrong! My mother, drunk or sober.)

Admirals—particularly *new* admirals—also have a reputation for being mean-tempered but goodhearted, loud spoken but taciturn, overworked yet involved in extraneous projects, technically experienced but internationally unaware, broad-minded but narrow-visioned, discontented but busily employed, overly demanding but easily satisfied, generally conservative but emotionally volatile, widely traveled but unadventurous, well-educated but salty-languaged, legislatively partisan but politically inactive, adamant but attentive and, above all, oversensitive to the suggestions of seniors and undersensitive to the recommendations of juniors.

These factors suggest that the plum assignment as an admiral's aide might have a rather large and bitter pit. In fact, except for the privilege of wearing the specially braided shoulder strands which signify this exalted position, an admiral's aide has little to look forward to except a seventy-hour week, a daily shower of wrath, a home life which consists of brief laundry visits, increased financial indebtedness (an aide always ends up settling tabs and tips), confused appointment schedules, and a life which, fantasy-like, encloses him within that unesthetic, unrealistic, and unelastic web of "cars and caramel candies." Significantly, those blue and gold aiguillettes which the aide so proudly wears have been more thoughtfully designed than one first imagines. One aide confessed that in an emergency he was sure that they could be used to hang himself from a short rafter. This, however, was the raving of a man who had been an aide for over three years. It is doubtful that a scientific stress analysis would confirm this theory.

36

Aides, of course, usually receive exceptionally fine fitness reports. Their personal ratings are really glowing tributes to their competence and, in most cases, are richly deserved. No one works harder or longer, on more frustratingly trivial tasks, under greater professional pressure, for such poor pay, in the employ of so unpleasant an individual, while surrounded by a never-ending burden of uncoordinated chaos as these modern water carriers for the Navy's thin blue line.

Unfortunately, however, the finely written paeans which aides receive from admirals reportedly are not considered overly valuable as performance indicators by any other officers, especially the more jaundiced-eyed members of promotion boards. Some believe they are eulogies. Therefore, there seems to be some basis for the recurring aide complaint that the admirals who preside over promotion boards have usually so overrated their own aides that they refuse to take seriously the written comments of their colleagues on any other aide. This has resulted, so says the "Aides' Union," in a rather poor professional forecast for many an officer's career.

In brief, the Navy attitude often is, "Is this young man worthy of promotion in spite of the fact that he was an admiral's aide?" For no comprehensible reason at all, aides, like drug addicts, are considered as subjects for rehabilitation only after long disassociation with their habit—and then only in isolated cases.

But I Just Bought You a New Nuclear Boat Last Year

May I pray thee to use thy scrupulous custom of searching out the verity.

Sir Walter Scott

Studies, under the guise of realistic analysis, often replace *solutions* which—no matter how obvious—will not be implemented as long as they are financially or politically unpalatable. For example, nuclear surface ships, which typify the practical application of technical progress within the U.S. Navy, are not being built. But, for two decades, they have been "studied." No amount of common sense on this subject will be tolerated, at least until a time arrives when the United States is forced to flush the irrationalities of an oil burning Navy down the drain of maritime history.

It will do little good to reiterate the arguments for a complete nuclear Navy. Visionary leadership, on this subject, lacks a 20/20 ocular guide. Simply stated, however, since 1960 no warship over eight thousand tons really should have been planned without nuclear propulsion. Naval officers know this, and our civilian leaders know this; yet, at the same time, discretion demands that no one can afford to admit he knows it.

This denial of objective truth, no matter how well-meaning the financial principle, is intellectually dishonest. Navy leaders particularly must find themselves in a profoundly disturbing position when they testify to the value of conventionally powered capital ships. At least they should be disturbed. Fortunately, coming to terms with professional honesty is a common trait among the military. Advertising those terms to the American public, however, seems to be promotionally hazardous. Basically, the problem today is mistaking consensus for reason or, to be even more brutal, substituting compromise for objectivity. Too many Navy leaders concentrate on apologizing for their parochialism instead of proclaiming their competence.

There also are tremendous emotional overtones to the arguments for a nuclear navy—just as there are personal involvements, to a lesser extent, for all-purpose military aircraft and missiles with nuclear engines. Of course the advocates of strategic bombers, faster fighter aircraft, vertical envelopment forces, guided missile programs, etc., are also violent verbal defenders of their causes; but the deep controversy concerning nuclear warships (forever afflicting the top military and civilian echelons) seems to have exceeded the normal Pentagon limits for charismatically controlled chaos.

Navy historians recall that the change from sail to coal plodded the same dreary path before verity vanquished vacillation. Coal was dirty, machinery unreliable, living conditions noisy, ships more expensive, overseas fueling stations unavailable, manpower requirements excessive, and the ponderous stacks—compared to the clean white sails of a four-masted man o' war—most unesthetic. Many nautical puritans made their point well; and they vocally, if not logically, delayed constructive progress. Fortunately the practical decisions of international neighbors induced the United States to furl its sails. Perhaps it also will require intense foreign competition or visible danger to move America's nuclear ship construction program off bottom dead center.

Additionally, anyone who has participated in or ever planned an ocean combat operation knows that the difference between success and failure often must depend on well coordinated refueling schedules—the black albatross which hangs around the neck of every attack carrier striking force. With nuclear power, plus additional emergency combat food and ammunition storage spaces, the Navy could make a quantum jump in its seapower posture—particularly in an age which requires dispersed sea formations.

There is little use in building such ships, of course, unless concurrent planning is done in the field of clean-lined, above-deck construction. Also, resupply and replacement items should be common among ships of the same basic design; this latter program, however, has been partially initiated. Additionally, every airplane that does not burn jet fuel should be banished to the beach, and future engine designs (jet and turboprop) should be directed toward a common fuel for all aircraft carrier planes. Those incidental forests also help to block Washington's view of the trees.

Another problem in the nuclear construction program for surface ships is that present operational plans are not oriented toward this posture. Unfortunately, less Delphic projects are underway for "fast logistic ships" (a jolly misnomer, invented to appease no one), single-screw destroyers, and conventional aircraft carriers. It is discouraging to see funds committed to these non-nuclear hulks when their object is to meet future fleet requirements. This affinity for handy obsolescence is not typical of all Navy or civilian managed projects, but the fact that professional acceptance of this archaic building program exists is, in itself, appalling. Some officers argue that anything is better than nothing, but this nursery school wisdom does little to restore a taxpayer's faith in marine humanity.

What is needed is a dynamic, long-term, nuclear-powered, surface ship construction program that divorces itself from the current curator attitude of neatly presiding over the remains of ancient ruins merely because they once were to be admired. This would require economies, perhaps for many years, in order to budget for the more expensive nuclear fleet. It would also require the Navy to agree to a decrease in gross ship numbers and this, too, would be difficult. As previously mentioned, many people believe that two of anything must be better than one of something else. This assumption, of course, must be rapidly abandoned. Grab bag logic has already hampered the Navy for over two decades, and the cheap mortgage of a larger, oil-powered fleet will someday prove to be a very poor bargain—at any price.

The Missile Milieu

I'd rather have an inch of dog than miles of pedigree.

Dana Burnet

Military missiles, like Gaul, are generally divided into three parts, one of which the propulsion system inhabits, a second which houses the guidance gadgets, and a third which contains the explosive charge.

In the early fifties, this basic format was taken into various caves by dedicated monks in order that they might develop individual strains of missiles, each containing singularly secret formulas. The avowed purpose of these industrial monastics seemed to be to prevent other non-religious orders from duplicating their product. Strangely, this uncooperative system was, in the early days of missilery, very successful. In a short period of time everyone was building beautiful, esoteric missiles without the least concern about what their colleagues were doing. It was sort of a Big Bullet Age. Everybody was making ammunition, but no one worried about the caliber.

At present there is a modicum of management over the missile industry, but there is also the danger—as second and third generation missiles develop—that even today's designers are inclined to sneak back into those caves again.

A "next generation" missile, of course, means that a company which conceives and develops a "Fragette" missile meets further and future competition by bringing out a line of newer and more powerful Fragettes; otherwise, government contracts will go to a more hustling organization. This leads to the serial era where industry, emulating Hollywood, produces not only Fragette, but Son of Fragette, Fragette and His Friends, Fragette Goes to Normal School, and the like.

If the Fragette is an air to surface missile, there is usually an industrial ground swell to modify Fragette so that it can become

41

an air to air, surface to surface, surface to air, underwater to moon, or any other all-purpose device which will keep the International Fragette Company in the fore of the Great Missile Age. Stockholders weep with glee over this technique. Meanwhile other companies are planning their "Better than Fragette" or "Anti-Fragette" missiles. This has been going on ever since the longbow and the crossbow were competitors. Both, as history records, made money.

The military services are the users of missile weapons. This is mentioned only to emphasize an incidental fact that was often ignored in the earlier days. As a result of this oversight the services had to assign missile czars who could at least recognize chaos even if they were almost powerless to control it. Today, however, new internal organizations within the military community are fully staffed to review, report, and document missile developments and programs. As a result, the services have attained a state of administrative control unique in the history of mankind—never before has so much confusion been so thoroughly managed. The Navy, naturally, has had its share of this generously distributed grief.

Shipboard missiles, for example, can be handled about as gracefully as boosting a pregnant cow over a barbed wire fence. New sea replenishment and transfer systems have surmounted some obstacles, but storage space and loading mechanisms still present particular problems. The missile industry, in its kindly way, has allowed the Navy to acknowledge the problems.

One answer would be to design shipboard systems so that they would accommodate only one basic missile container. This has been accomplished with notable success in Polaris submarines. Surface ship missiles, as weapon purpose dictates, would require interchangeable warheads, guidance systems, propellent chambers, and "dummy" sections which could, when combined in below deck assembly plants, evolve as the same sized weapon, fired by a common launcher, regardless of target. A long-range weapon, needing more propellent would not have to sacrifice either guidance or weapon capability, but the dummy package would differ from a short-range weapon's dummy package in order to meet the basic length, weight, and dimension criteria.

American industry and military technology could solve these shipboard missile problems in precisely such a standardized manner if someone were given the authority to plan, program, budget, and direct such a project. He would need a machete, however, rather than a stilletto, for every hawker in the missile weapon trade would beg an exception for his birds.

This is not to say that we do not have good shipboard missiles, although some would allow that we do not have great ones. It is only that the diaper days should be over for the missile industry, but nobody wants the job of potty training.

Designs for shipboard missiles also must be directed toward common size assembly, loading, transfer, carriage, and launching systems—and those who cannot stand the competitive heat should get out of the industrial kitchen. The military, of course, is partly at fault, for they have tried to coordinate leadership with industry, while industry was honestly searching for direction. Coordinated leadership, since Adam, has usually proven futile.

Specific atomic warheads cannot be discussed, but their privileged status does not make them immune to criticism. The United States has enough atomic weapons to accomplish everything editorialists and official spokesmen have said they can accomplish, but they also suffer from the non-standardization principle which, though justifiable in the experimental days, now results in a bloody expense. Short-term justification, unfortunately, is a platform on which too many officers of all services have built successful careers.

Atomic weapons are part of the United States Navy's arsenal, and if they are missile launched they must be made to meet future shipboard missile standards. The current polyglot of choice liquors is admirable, but the Navy can get the same punch from raw moonshine—at one hell of a lower price.

If someone would only correlate the story of David and Goliath with the shipboard missile systems, a wee bit of sanity might prevail. The Navy must launch its stones, atomic or conventional, from slings—and it is basically senseless to expend sums of other people's money on stones of varied sizes and slings of diversified tensile strength. All the Navy now needs, after twenty years of technical tremors, is to choose its standard shipboard system, specify its requirements, announce its criteria, allow time for reclamas and, for the sake of the American taxpayers, *get on with it!*

Where, Oh Where Has My Little Sub Gone?

And what tune is it ye pull to men?

Herman Melville

The clear and definitive analysis of underwater sound signals is about as reliable an aural science as identifying cricket chirps with an ear trumpet in a herd of stampeding elephants.

This interesting challenge occurs because of the indefinite patterns which exist in all oceans due to the variations in salinity, temperature, currents, surface structure, pressure depths, sea floor topography, ambient noise level, ship traffic, and the like. It is not that these obstacles are incalculable, but only that the physics and mechanics of exactly identifying and locating a specific underwater sound, at extreme ranges, makes the construction of atomic weapons seem like a Tinker Toy project.

Despite the complexity and security involved, it is not too revealing to mention that the Navy is forging ahead with the technical phonic solutions to these problems and has made considerable progress in developing effective underwater sound recognition and reception devices. Of course the Navy has wrestled with this alligator for about fifty years, and by now the Navy's sonar operators well recognize the difference between "a dead whale and a stove boat!" But it is also obvious that until some technological echo barrier is broken, such as the invention of a space age underwater radar, long-range sound reception (accompanied by a computer system for immediate sonic analysis) will remain as the paramount problem. Investigation, therefore, must proceed with reasonable haste in that direction.

There are two specific steps which would improve the existing underwater surveillance system and thereby provide an integrated oceanic early warning network similar in scope to the North

American radar warning project. The first step is to implant carefully a more extensive fixed hydrophone system on the ocean floors. Specific installation points must remain classified, but a complex Atlantic and Pacific sound grid is recommended generally. Nuclear attack submarines also could be added to provide the mobile force necessary to plug any sonic gaps in this hydrophonic dike.

The second step would be to tie this network together at a national underwater command center where the latest analytic techniques and high speed signal interpretation devices could provide information, on secure circuits, to operational force commanders.

Following the initial reports of foreign submarine activity, the tracking stations would continue to provide bearing information to the command center and, with a sufficient number of cross reference lines, a continuous plot could be maintained of both routine and potential threat activity under nearby waters.

Special teams, under the direct control of operational or area commanders, could be alerted to track and identify submarines, whenever necessary. These special patrols for underwater reconnaissance tasks (SPURT) should consist of turboprop patrol aircraft, nuclear attack submarines, and nuclear surface destroyers, as well as newly developed hydrofoils and air-cushion vehicles. Coordinated SPURT training in search, localization, and attack procedures would be practiced against all classes of friendly submarines to achieve a high degree of efficiency under relatively silent operating conditions.

Since some sound reception centers would be located abroad, the personnel manning the overseas surveillance stations should be rotated about every three months to identically equipped United States stations where their families would remain located. Additionally, the required overseas facilities should be modest in size and remote (some of the more massive bases now seem to attract growing hordes of itinerant professional rioters who lead placard pageants around the installations). In this instance, American enthusiasm for organizational growth should be contained. If three people in a relatively inaccessible overseas area can do the job, any affinity for expanded staffs or city living should be discouraged.

45

The Fixed Base Concept of Patrol Aviation

Pessimism, when you get used to it,
Is just as agreeable as optimism.

Enoch Bennet

The advent of the P-3 Orion aircraft as the world's best airborne antisubmarine warfare (ASW) weapons platform was not accompanied by a smidgen of advanced tactical thought concerning ASW air operations. The P-3, a four engine, turbojet, electronic marvel, deployed overseas in the same philosophical time frame as its circa 1945 predecessors; it also patrolled the same ancient tracks, photographed the same motley commerical ships and, in general, stumbled after its simulated submarine enemy in the same clumsy way as its Smithsonian ancestors. Enthusiasm and vision did not accompany mechanical progress!

Few individuals fought to equate the new plane's operational flexibility with anything other than the archaic movement principles and limited submarine hunting capabilities which inhibited earlier ASW aircraft. The same attitude prevailed when the automobile replaced the horse. No one knew what to do about this quantum jump other than to comment, in passing, that there really wasn't any change since the engine was still up front—and that's where the horse was!

Other reasons that the P-3's excellent equipment seldom approached its operational potential were that the fixed principles of sea-shore rotation prevented trained crews from remaining together; the two year (often less) system of transferring officers out of squadrons devoured plane commander talent as fast as it was produced; and the many non-ASW missions allowed few periods for training squadron personnel in an ASW environment. Those omitted tactical ASW training missions were, after all, the avowed primary reason for a patrol squadron's existence. So when opportunities did arise, too many crews sallied forth after submarines in the spastic manner which President Wilson, a half century ago, described as, "hunting hornets all over the farm."

Of course the haphazard system of transferring officer and enlisted personnel in and out of ASW squadrons, which our allied friends abhor, is still the paramount problem; it gives patrol aviation about as much stability as a greased pig on a waxed slide. A more sensible use of senior pilots in patrol aviation would also help, for although youth is an undeniable asset in fighter and attack aviation, there is no indication in the study of safety records or operational performance results that young plane commanders are more capable of performing ASW tasks than the more experienced, older pilots. Patrol aviation advocates, however, seem to have learned relatively little from the older pilot records of either the airlines or the military transport squadrons. As with the bachelor who contends against marriage, Navy aviation enthusiasts who argue against airline procedures may be right, but their lack of experience tends to diminish the weight of their argument.

Expanding Orion squadrons from nine to twelve aircraft, with a captain in charge and commander aviators as plane commanders, also might not improve things, but it seems to be worth trying. Now ASW aviation is often only an advanced training command for youngsters who jump into civilian airline schools as soon as their obligated naval service expires.

The Navy does not have the number of P-3 Orions nor, for that matter, any other aircraft, ships, trained personnel, or junior career officers that it wants and needs. It never did, and it never will. But the Navy can use its available men and ASW aircraft in a more rational manner. For example, the P-3 aircraft is a prime example of the ragged staff tail wagging a well groomed operational dog. A desk-bound fleet air wing staff commander, as every P-3 squadron commander knows, is the more senior of the two. Doubts about this are usually clarified with minimal trauma. This means that the P-3 Orion has been tactically employed and deployed in accordance with the plans of the fleet air wing commanders—and their seniors. Some of these plans, unfortunately, have shown about as much originality, enterprise, and drive as a hibernating sloth.

It is not entirely the fault of the non-operational staff decision makers, for many P-3 squadron officers themselves have refused to be dragged out of their cockpit lethargy. In other words, it would take an exhaustive search to locate written recommenda-

47

tions by experienced P-3 aviators which outlined original tactical programs for the deployment and operation of the new plane.

The P-3 then, has continued to subsist on the old fare of fixed base operations, merchant shipping tracks, hourly voice reports, radar flooding, and limited ASW training. While not entirely obsolete, this grandmotherly system has been in effect for over twenty years. If the ASW effort in patrol aviation is not soon modified to keep pace with the potential enemy submarine progress, these Currier and Ives oriented doctrines may survive for another two decades. It is almost as if the technological changes since 1950 have been purposely ignored, although observed as interesting phenomena. Too many military men in decision making positions within ASW aviation remain as fixed in habit as the old New Englander who, when asked if he had seen many changes in his time, answered, "Yes, and I've been against every one of them."

It does not take a tactical genius to see that there is no logical reason for commencing area patrols from the same fixed points overseas year after year. If, for reasons more politic than strategic, some remote overseas routes must be flown interminably, they should originate from different geographic landmarks and arrive at check point coordinates at random times. In addition, patrols should generally be conducted silently with position reports, for safety purposes, broadcast only on a secure network every two or three hours. The current system of constant radio babble alerts even a simulated enemy submarine to an aircraft's position long before the plane can locate the target. This verbal Niagara, when combined with continued electronic radiations, puts the element of a surprise attack at sea in the same category as an unnoticed pregnancy in a small town.

In addition, the enthusiasm for submarine pursuit diminishes as the number of surface quarries increases, and the boring hunt for merchant ships, "let's see which crew can photograph forty oilers this week," depletes the modest stock of ASW crew incentive. The junior officers and enlisted men come to patrol aviation in the belief that antisubmarine warfare is a concentrated, almost full time effort. The rude awakening, combined with their relatively short tour and their constant crew shifts, does not generate that pride of effort which the men and aircraft so rightly deserve. These issues, combined with unrealistic deployment schedules, unnecessary administrative burdens overseas, the snail's pace of adopting airborne operational data processing techniques, and the relatively low pay provided for the Navy technicians who are expected to repair, operate, and interpret sophisticated electronic equipment have allowed airborne ASW to become less effective an arm of America's naval might than the nation should reasonably expect.

Specifically, the P-3 Orion aircraft has such flexibility that, with proper planning, an entire squadron can deploy almost anywhere in the world in 24 hours. For the sake of a reasonably settled military family life (families remain at home during deployments), there is no reason why squadron tours overseas should not now be made for three or four months rather than the current rate of six or seven months—especially if personnel rotation programs were also set up on a more sane basis. This might, in turn, mean that the Navy would have to be organized on a more functional line in its operational forces overseas, and this is anathema to many air wing staffs—even if logic supports the change.

ASW squadrons also should vary their deployment areas throughout the world in order to get a little cross-pollination from working in all of the earth's ocean areas. American ASW tactical crews would profit by the experience of coordinating their ASW efforts and oceanographic knowledge with their colleagues in other nations. The British, Japanese, Australian, and Canadian crews, to name only a few, use airborne ASW procedures which can best be understood, modified, or adopted to the Navy's needs through operational participation with friends.

The P-3 and its siblings must also be accompanied by new concepts of rapid mobility rather than the nesting urge which typifies the fleet air wing system. Past mental reservations required the Navy to provide a cosy home for patrol planes to and from their assigned missions; and these transit limitations, in turn, evolved from sincere anxiety over safety margins and operational risk factors. These perimeters can now be drastically expanded, but only if the fleet air wing apron strings are cut.

There is also a definite international advantage in getting these P-3 Orions into such areas as the Norwegian Sea, the Malacca Strait, the Bay of Bengal, ad infinitum, more frequently. This posture would establish a concomitant naval power aura over the U. S. merchant fleet. This worldwide projection of patrol aviation is necessary if the United States is to maintain an image of quiet presence on the high seas. Such an image, incidentally, is well noted among the mariners of other nations who labor on and under the oceans of the world. Not any presuppositions of power, no matter how well documented, are worth the vellum they are printed on unless the submarine, warship, and merchant skippers of the world actually see United States aircraft at sea over both those busy and remote ocean routes which carry the substance of most human effort—international trade.

A new airborne antisubmarine warfare and ocean surveillance program, however, must be more than a rambling operation or a singular experiment. Under the auspices of our OAS, NATO, SEATO and ANZUS friends, and from the fields of other allies with whom we have mutual security pacts, patrol aircraft could, in the next decade, become a force capable of sweeping over the world's seas in peace and sanitizing America's ocean approaches in the event of conflict. To do this, however, patrol aviation must break many bonds with which it has, to some extent, tied itself for over twenty years. Most of all, the fixed-base concept must be abandoned if the Navy is to effect a global ASW posture, rather than a provincial one. The ASW hunter has for too many years remained near the hearth, and that is not, in the words of today's teenagers, "where the action is."

The Naval War College— *Viribus Mari Victoria*

I have great affection for the bridge which carried me over.

William E. Borah

The United States Naval War College in Newport, Rhode Island, is the senior service college in the military, having been in existence since 1884. It has suffered through constant neglect and adversity ever since Captain Mahan once smuggled coal past the budget-conscious Navy hierarchy just to keep the chill off the granite about 1890. Ironically, recent War College presidents have had to smuggle education to the Navy—a less dramatic but nevertheless as severe a battle.

The problem is to enroll sufficient students and qualified staff officers to justify the school's existence. The lack of students, as always, exists because the Navy must man ships, squadrons, and an ever increasing mass of shore duty billets before releasing officers for one year of advanced training. The solution, as always, is to defer the problem.

During and after each war, there is an initial surge of enthusiasm for peacetime education. This results from the shock of not having enough well-informed and capably trained senior officers in operational and planning staffs. Unfortunately the impetus provided by the postwar argument—Why in hell weren't we better prepared?—soon degenerates into the assignment officer's wail— How can we shortchange understaffed commands just to provide students? The cycle is tedious.

The staffing problem of the Naval War College suffers different and diverse obstacles than the student problem. First, many naval officers feel that their selection for a teaching assignment on the War College staff is similar to the careful examination of the infected for transportation to leper colonies. The poor selec-

51

tion record of Naval War College staff officers for higher rank seems to confirm this negative reaction. In fact, the low staff officer promotion rate in most Navy schools has never built a glorious addition to the ark of the Navy's advancement covenant.

Additionally, the concept of using officers with advanced degrees in a teaching capacity at The Naval War College, which is a noble idea, never has been implemented. The military officers, therefore, can more accurately be described as a staff than a faculty, since the officers who are involved with the students often act only as briefing specialists, team leaders, curriculum writers, general advisors, charity campaign coordinators, pamphlet distributors, and program directors.

It is not that these paper work tasks and orientation drills are unimportant or that they could be left undone but rather, if Naval War College staff officers are not used as lecturers and instructors in the art and science of military operations and associated lore, there really is no need to require the assignment of so many knowledgeable and capable officers with Master's degrees which the College emphatically demands for this mythical faculty duty.

The Naval War College officers, both staff and students, also suffer from the absolute inability of the Navy to tie its promotion, command selection, and educational systems into one package. (The U. S. Army, incidentally, has better evaluated these relationships.) Some student officers of commander rank who are sent to the Naval War College are subsequently *not* selected for promotion to captain shortly after their arrival. Thus, their enthusiasm for training is noticeably diminished. This often cements a discouraging staff-student relationship. The question then arises, "Why was I so carefully chosen for the Naval War College?" The answer, of course, is that the staff and students are not as carefully chosen as they should be. The effect, however, is to damage the reputation of the College, de-emphasize its importance within the Navy, and to forever convince some student officers (lieutenant commanders) that they should steer clear of future assignments to the NWC staff to avoid promotional warts.

Until the Navy can assign more officers as students at the Naval War College, it should at least screen more effectively those who do attend. With the prestige and stature of the senior naval school, there should be a requirement that the promotion of every individual, in either a staff or student capacity, be reasonably assured at the time of his Newport assignment. It is not enough that these officers are good bets for promotion, or that their records indicate they should be promoted. What is needed is certification by the school selection board that barring an untoward incident, such as leading riots at the Newport Jazz Festival, these officers *will* be promoted. If such assurance cannot be given, the officers in question should not be sent to the Naval War College and, if the combination of promotion, command selection, and educational assignment potential is beyond the capacity of the current administrative structure in Washington, the structure should and must be changed. The result of one NWC student gaining a command without subsequent promotion, another gaining promotion without command, and a third achieving neither does little to enhance the stature of the Naval War College and nothing to justify the theory of a coherent officer personnel planning policy within the Department of the Navy.

Currently, there are two major courses for U. S. military officers at the Naval War College, the junior course at the Naval Command and Staff College and the senior course at the Naval Warfare College, neither of which are required to guarantee promotional success.

The junior course at the Naval Command and Staff College is an excellent but by no means complete method of preparing lieutenant commanders for the duties specified in the school's title. For example, if an officer is fortunate enough to be assigned command of a ship or squadron after graduation, he really has not had specific training in the administrative, personnel, judicial, or technical problems which he will encounter as a commanding officer. If assigned as a staff officer, however, he will receive some valuable apprentice work. Incidentally, the recent promotion statistics for students of this junior school (but not the staff) have been encouraging. Lieutenant commander students in the junior course are almost assured of commander status.

The senior course at the Naval Warfare College neither examines the history of naval warfare nor explores comparative military strategies in detail. What it does accomplish is to train officers for senior joint and unified staff assignments. This is a valuable goal, but the more parochial idea of doing nautical things in a progressive way normally leaps to a student's mind when he receives his orders to the Naval Warfare College. In his subsequent studies he is not particularly encouraged, as you might suspect, to complete this leap.

Students in the junior school have complained that their

53

course resembles the Navy's Line School—which it did. But the Navy has closed its Line School, thus stifling that unsolicited line of attack. Some senior students also have declared that their school too closely approaches the junior course. This argument, of course, could be choked off by not sending such thankless critics to the senior course if they have attended the junior one—thus severing their source of experienced opinion.

There is also a restless feeling that everything taught in the two schools really could be combined into one ten-month curriculum. This, however, is pure heresy except among those students who have attended both courses and whisper cogently in academic corners.

Perhaps, more importantly, the Naval War College staff needs an input of newly selected commanders and captains to replace the already discouraged with the hopefully enthusiastic. Also, the retention on the staff of those commanders who have been denied promotion to captain, and the quiet pasturing of captains who know that their careers have a terminal diagnosis, dulls the lustre of the entire academic image. This is not to say that non-promoted officers are not fine men nor capable staff members, but only that the Naval War College is a ridiculous place to assign them. Their generators are basically not supplying the intellectual power which is needed to brighten the students' lamps, and their facial reaction to progressive ideas is about the same as if they had bitten into a raw clam sandwich.

Familiarity Can Also Breed Affection

The rank is but the guinea's stamp.

Robert Burns

In today's Navy it is rare to find an officer who is very personally attached to the enlisted men who serve with him. Too often the chaplain, already overburdened with crises, chaos, and charitable campaigns, is the only human repository available for the anxieties, anguish, and anger which infest most young men at one time or another during the early days of their Navy careers; but it is the enlisted men's division officer who should be more involved.

Conversely, a few young division officers who mistake popularity for leadership are inclined to over-socialize with their men when on liberty to justify their severe, exact, and aloof standards during working hours. This reverse psychology is neither notably successful nor professionally valid. It is not that an officer's camaraderie or drinking capacity is unappreciated by enlisted men, but the men soon lose confidence in anyone who employs a double standard in his relationships.

These dual postures—of either professional indifference or private indulgence—are responsible, at least in part, for the low re-enlistment rate of many first-term sailors. This observation is not meant to diminish the ever-present effects of poor pay and arduous sea duty on re-enlistment, but only to amplify the signal that has been generated by many young men in the Navy (as well as other segments of American society) that, "no one really cares."

It is increasingly hard to find officers who know the personal backgrounds, family life, future plans, and troublesome times of their enlisted men. Many do not even know of their enlisted personnel's marital state and, on rare occasions, are even ignorant of the names of men serving in their department or division.

55

On the positive side, there still are a few division officers who keep personal notebooks which contain data on the sailors in their division, together with the names of their enlisted men's parents, wives, and children—and even the children's birth dates. But this information, so readily accessible to a division officer, usually is ignored. Yet, in retrospect, this small element of personal knowledge is perhaps the most important collateral asset of every good officer, for without it an officer's pose of sincere concern over an enlisted man during an individual crisis is a sham. For example, feeble attempts to discover what caused a breach of discipline, after the fact, often have uncovered a bonanza of ignorance concerning the man on the part of his division officer. In this instance the division officer's historical lament, "I don't know, sir; but I'll find out," is as embarassing as a submarine on a sand bar.

One of the many reasons that officers currently do not have this real attachment to their men is that the Navy discourages positive relationships. Captains expect and encourage personal confidences between the chaplains and the men; instead, they really should deplore the fact that it is the chaplain and not the department head or division officer who has taken control of many of the tasks which rightly fall under the leadership guidon. Turenne said, "You must love soldiers in order to understand them, and understand them in order to lead them." Obviously both tenets require that you must first know them, and intimate knowledge of enlisted men is not a common trait in naval officers today.

A division officer who honestly states to the captain that, "I didn't realize that the man had family problems; in fact, I didn't even know he was married," should be barred from making recommendations concerning this man's punishment. If a division officer has such a limited knowledge of the fundamentals of leadership, it is doubtful that he will be blessed with rare disciplinary insight.

Throughout history all great generals had this insight and, though they were exceptionally stern when their hard corps regulations were violated, they also were exceptionally close to their men throughout their careers and unmoved by petty charges against veteran fighters whenever legal nonsense appeared. (When two of Napoleon's veterans were brought into his presence for stealing grapes from the Emperor's vineyard, Napoleon merely dismissed them with the advice, "wait until they are ripe.") This ability of military leaders to weigh values, maintain control, and judge combat troops requires close officer-enlisted relationships, personal attachments, objective appraisals, and a fine measure of compassion. And those elements need not prejudice either leadership or discipline; in fact, they allow these factors to function more effectively. But the key, of course, is the professional experience which derives from each officer's familiarity with the prospects and problems of every enlisted man who serves with him (not under him). It is not achieved by osmosis.

Additionally, it is not enough for an officer just to make an effort to know his men. He must *concern* himself with them! Occasional knowledge, like occasional virtue, does not imply any long-range values. Division officers particularly should have detailed information on every enlisted man in their division and should carefully brief their successors on each individual sailor. Today's too-rapid turnover of officer personnel in fleet units is an inherent obstacle to any personnel stability program, but until assignment policies permit long-term affiliations, each unit commander at least should attempt to initiate the closest officer-enlisted relationships which are possible in his command under the present circumstances. Though fiction writers find it far-fetched, officers and enlisted men have been known to like each other.

The professional measure of a division officer today also has become less and less related to the way he runs his division. Often the department head is held responsible for work schedules, the legal officer for discipline, the chaplain for morale, the commanding officer for leadership, the education officer for training, the career counselor for reenlistment, and the executive officer for the annual all hands' picnic. These assumed assignments obviously leave the division officer with very little personal responsibility for his men. In fact, he really is now denied many of the opportunities to meet, counsel, and concern himself with the very functions which should be in his domain. Therefore, since he is no longer assigned primary responsibility for the actions of his enlisted men, nor graded according to his relationships with them, it is understandable (though disappointing) that the division officer often does not even try to fuse his character or instill a unit spirit into his group. More importantly, the personal attachment which could and should exist between the division officer and his men has been destroyed by such organizational diversification. This spread pattern of responsibility, incidentally, was planned originally to benefit enlisted men, but there are indications that this pillar-to-post policy may have been responsible for placing them in that limbo where "no one really cares."

Astronauts and Aquanauts

And while I at length debate and beat the bush,
There shall step in other men and catch the
birds.

John Heywood

Almost one hundred years ago the British ship *Challenger* completed a three and one-half year oceanographic research venture which was dedicated to probing the mysteries of the world's seas. Relatively speaking, in terms of advanced technology, the United States has not added more than a postscript to that epic.

Today's splendor, drama, and recorded noise, which accompanies America's space program, is presented live and in brilliant peacock hues on television. The dull, drab, and often seasick routine of oceanography is not given equal or, thankfully, as colorful coverage. Less wisely, however, the seascape is not accorded a proportionate amount of the national budget.

America's oceanographers, and their scientific seaborne colleagues, are perhaps superior in knowledge to those of any nation—at least in theoretical arenas. The Russians, however, are placing an increasing emphasis on practical work. Today they far surpass all nations in the quality and quantity of research vessels which are scurrying about that seventy per cent of the earth's surface so dear to the hearts of sixth-grade geography teachers and naval officers.

If only half of the money that the United States has spent getting a man to the moon could be directed gradually toward ocean research over a ten-year period, American leadership under the seas would be unchallenged. Private companies have already added to the nation's wealth by discovering oil reserves on the continental shelf. But there is much more. It seems reasonable that underwater mining, off-shore fish hatcheries, desalinization projects, earthquake sensor systems, ocean defense programs, submarine transportation methods, sea communications research, and deep-water fish harvests from that other, wetter world would benefit mankind equally as well as a jaunt to luna land.

The craters of the moon, which stimulate the minds of the adventurous, present a trivial panorama compared to the earth's ocean floor. Under these world seas are gorges which make the Grand Canyon seem like a dry gulch, mountains rivaling the Himalayas, and rivers along the ocean's floor so wide and long and deep that the Mississippi, by comparison, would appear as a stingy stream.

The sea and space, then, are still the real unconquered worlds. Man's efforts will someday allow him to vanquish both. But until a major break-through can be made in propulsion systems, the cost of space research will soon outweigh the results which mankind hopes to gain. The moon program is valuable, but farther fields must net more than repeated or even refined data if any country's economy is to justify a space program. After nations have visited the moon a few times, it will be both difficult and foolhardy to attempt further excursions at the expense of human needs. Hopefully some parts of the moon will be flaked with golden sand or even gouda cheese, but if they are not, research funds would be better directed toward basic engine, fuel, and capsule technology than toward tourism.

The oceans' unseen landscape, however, promises more than secrets. While the sea does have its mysterious depths to enchant the dreamer, it also has food for the hungry, work for the unemployed, resources for the producer, water for the deserts, mineral wealth for the manufacturer, and unlimited power for those nations having the patience, energy, courage, and fiscal faith necessary to wring it dry.

It is not unlikely that America's undersea oil reserves may someday exceed her territorial ones; perhaps her entire strategic defensive and offensive military systems will be located outside of the continental limits; her submarine fishing fleets might supply the bulk of the world's seafood; minerals might be processed more quickly from her flanking oceans than from her Western mines; and her drought afflicted areas might become only a matter of recorded history. This is the potential of that vast uncharted world. It cannot be realized without the visions and leadership of men who have the financial power to direct an ocean program and the courage of others willing to challenge an environment as hostile and unyielding (but much less glamorous) as that which has been probed by their colleagues in the clouds.

Please, Josephine, Don't Go Near That Machine

There is nothing as terrifying as ignorance in action.

Goethe

Not long ago a very senior U.S. Air Force officer suggested to a knowledgeable military audience that the Navy should send drone helos (unmanned helicopters) into Vietnam combat zones to rescue personnel behind enemy lines. This sounded logical to almost everyone except those Navy officers who had been affiliated for years with drones during the destroyer antisubmarine helicopter (DASH) program's formative years. These officers were so badly and visibly shaken by the naive suggestion of rescue drones that their subsequent conversation was almost incoherent.

The DASH was just such an unmanned, and often unmanageable, machine. It submerged (without design) into the oceans of the world with regularity for so many years that its flight characteristics are considered about as graceful as the ascent of a pregnant ostrich.

The DASH has been historically subject to such nervous command decisions as—"Don't let it out of sight," "If it gets more than three miles from the ship, shoot the damn thing down," "Don't fly it when dependents are on board," "Leave it in the crate and don't mention it to me again, ever," and "Do not launch DASH within 75 miles of land!" (This made little sense, since DASH could fly 85 miles.)

The DASH, to the initiated, would be the last instrument of survival which a sane man would look to for solace. In fact, the mere presence of a robot-like, meandering rescue helicopter over a

60

position behind enemy lines might be more of a clue to the enemy than a haven of hope for someone attempting an escape.

Newer and more sophisticated models might improve the reliability of DASH, but the thought of an unmanned vehicle which had to make maneuvering decisions on the basis of enemy groundfire presumes a capability in art and science which is quite remote from the prosaic life of land combat (and survival).

Since DASH was launched at sea, most DASH crashes resulted in an unrecovered flight vehicle (newer models have flotation gear). This means that it has been extremely difficult to pinpoint the cause of accidents in the mass of paperwork reports which must accompany each lost bird. One officer suggested that the remarks should include the phrase, "it fall down and go boom!" He was not technically oriented.

Other negative aspects of the DASH program are that it takes a considerable length of time to prepare the bird for launching. It can even take an entire day if the commanding officer is an extremely cautious individual—one, say, who is reluctant to fill out accident reports. In this regard, an emotional constant often seems to enter into each drone operation whereby new skippers launch (and lose) their DASH vehicles with gay abandon. They then become old skippers and refuse to ever fly it again.

The enlisted men who run the DASH on destroyers are assigned to duty from the aviation ratings. This means that they now have become maternally bound to the surface Navy. This also means that they cannot get into squadron crews and draw their normally anticipated flight pay. These dewinged enlisted men, therefore, are less than enthusiastic about their loss of cash and, to be honest, often have only a modest interest in their jobs.

The overseer who sits in the destroyer's "chariot" and attempts to control the wayward movements and wanderlust of the vehicle is, conversely, a surface (non-aviation) officer. His throne has an electronic console with accompanying controls where he can sit on the exposed ship's fantail and tinker with his toy. However, a DASH officer's career also is fraught with despair. He ages visibly with each crash, and it doesn't improve his disposition when his drone is launched off the New England coast and heads for London—never to be seen again.

The DASH also has preempted a position of honor on some destroyers—it has taken over the spot previously reserved for showing movies. This crass act is akin to whittling on life boats in the minds of many sailors.

It must be admitted that the DASH, when ready, is one of the best and quickest antisubmarine reload systems aboard a destroyer at sea. Anyone who has had to shovel torpedoes up the Mark 32 launcher or has thought wistfully about trying to position a replacement antisubmarine rocket (ASROC) understands the reloading benefits of DASH.

It is significant, however, that the entire contingent of naval aviators refuse to take their planes into the same airspace where DASH is gyrating. DASH is, therefore, a lone ranger. And, like its western hero counterpart, its value in rescuing friends or fair maidens is pure fiction.

The Lieutenant, USN

Nothing's too good for our boys in the service!
(And that's what we'll give them.)

Anonymous

The Navy—as well as just about every other government organization—often finds itself temporarily short of something valuable. One constant and critical deficit is the lack of skilled manpower. In certain fields this gap can be bridged, either temporarily through crash reassignment programs, or permanently through such financial expedients as "proficiency pay" or bonuses for technically skilled enlisted men. The Achilles' heel, however, which has never been dipped into any river of balm, is the Navy's ever present junior pilot shortage.

Since the Navy will not use its senior pilots (age 35 and over) and will not pay junior aviators more than a modest fee to remain in the service, there is always this unfilled chasm. This ten year hiatus is with the Navy constantly, simply because it cannot retain enough junior aviators on active duty in the rank of lieutenant to fill the many cockpits which are available for these young flyers. Now, why can't the Navy keep them?

A lieutenant with four years of flying duty has fulfilled his obligated service to the nation. He may leave the Navy or remain, as he prefers. As a flyer he will receive, after four years of tenure, an additional one hundred sixty-five dollars a month incentive pay for his hazardous duty. After taxes, this amounts to about fifteen hundred dollars a year—hardly a munificent sum. In fact, it is less than a *month's* flight pay for a civilian airline captain. (Incidentally, one hundred sixty-five dollars is approximately the same amount of extra pay as the lieutenant's *father* received for flying as a Navy pilot when he was a lieutenant during World War II. Financial progress is not our most important product.)

The lieutenant also may have to leave home for overseas

flying duty about seven months each year. As expected, this deployment policy concerns his young wife and family considerably.

Even these negative constants, however, would not deter as many young men if additional factors were not so heavily weighed in favor of their mass decisions to leave the service.

First, one can be killed in naval aviation. This is, as poker players note, "just for openers." Second, the airlines pay much finer salaries, with a comparatively modest fatality record (if flying is a paramount consideration). Third, a family can be more permanently located, with a sense of relative security and a reasonable home life in almost any comparable civilian endeavor—including airline flying. Fourth, (and this is, admittedly, a singular example) a civilian airline captain can fly a four engine turboprop eighty hours a month (union rule maximum) for about twenty-five thousand dollars a year, while a patrol plane pilot (as a Navy lieutenant) will often fly the same aircraft in the Navy over one hundred hours a month for "peanuts."

Of course, no naval officer remains in the service for the express purpose of joining the affluent society. There are psychological and sociological benefits—or satisfactions—which must in fairness be related to every officer's commissioned status. He has, for example, a position of leadership. The problem is that the junior aviator is so involved with becoming a technician during his first four years (both by direction and as a matter of survival), that he has little opportunity to practice leadership, command, control, or even the direction of any other individual but himself. Therefore, his status as an officer and a leader of men is a moot point at best, and often irrelevant.

If the lieutenant transfers to a multi-engine training squadron after his first four years of military service he merely instructs newer and younger technicians, and it is not long before both he and his students realize that their special skill has a premium stamp which airline companies recognize more directly.

Another unfavorable pressure that the young pilot may feel, rightly or wrongly, is that he is not flying in a squadron that is in the best promotional position in the aviation pecking cycle. This heirarchy, though its existence often is vehemently denied, provides future promotion opportunities for a young tiger in the following approximate order.

VF — fighter pilots
VA — attack pilots
VAH — heavy attack pilots

64

VS	— antisubmarine warfare pilots
VP	— patrol pilots
HS	— helicopter pilots
VX	— experimental pilots
VQ	— reconnaissance pilots
VU	— utility pilots
VR	— transport pilots

There are other designators, as well as variations to this theme but, in general, long term success, higher rank and even *early* promotion from the *bottom* of the feed bin are difficult (read "impossible" below VS). Even within the structure, sub-structures exist—such as the best *type* of VF aircraft, the highest number of VF carrier landings (and even VF *night* carrier landings), etc. There is practically unlimited opportunity for professional snobism.

These are just some of the factors which the aviation lieutenant considers before he leaves the service. He may know or not know that civilian life has its own peculiar pits and pendulums. He does know, however, that he hasn't really had a chance to be in charge of anything—or to be home with his family—or to make much money, for over four years. If the Navy really has something to say to him, either financially or professionally, the aviation lieutenant feels that it has neglected to say it, or hasn't said it very well. Civilian organizations have been less reluctant in their propositions—and more rewarding in their offers.

How About
Collective Quarantines?

*Short cuts are always tempting when one feels
his cause is just. Short cuts have always been
justified on the grounds that the end being worthy, the means of reaching it are not important.
Short cuts, however, are dangerous. If they can
be taken against one person or group, they can
be taken against another.*

William O. Douglas

Many Navy officers still have an almost sentimental affection for the once powerful seapower operation known as "pacific
blockades." But pacific blockade is an anachronism if used as a
unilateral resort to economic pressure to force a contention. It is
instant coercion—the paradise of the nautically strong. It is also a
short cut to poor foreign relations. An obvious weakness is that it
may antagonize the state under blockade to the point where a
declaration of war soon abolishes the pacific portion of the whole
affair. Enforced pacificism and declared virtue somehow seem to
generate doubts.

The theory of pacific blockade has exceptional attraction,
however. It is theoretically bloodless, which appeals to the hu-
mane; it is done with a minimum of military force, which has an
attraction for economists and politicians; and it is imposed on the
sea, away from the sovereign territory of the offending state, which
results in an irresistible charm that soon ensnares statesmen and
naval advocates alike. If effected by one state against another
today, however, a modern unilateral pacific blockade could create
a world pool of treacle, only rivaled by the Great Boston Molasses
Flood.

66

Additionally, a hypothetically enforced and effective pacific blockade against a submissive state—which also must interdict ships of other states—subsumes that most nations have merchant fleets which would view the blockade with genial affability. This is most unlikely, for a pacific blockade, even if formed only to prevent the shuttling of contraband weapons, is bound to tread on some tender neutral hull, especially with the registration system which now exists for merchant vessels. It is common for nation X to register the bulk of its merchantmen under the flag of nation Y. Should the merchantmen of all nations be frisked? This basic corollary, at first glance, smacks of the doctrine that a little imperialism never hurts. But unilateral pacific blockades are fraught with exceptionally hazardous international problems which now render the concept impractical and, perhaps, irrelevant. For example, the poorest nations now have submarines and air power; the smallest states have United Nations representation and fraternal adherents to their sovereign aspirations; the members of regional agencies abhor individual enforcement action; and the world's merchantmen resent any infringement on their mobility.

These considerations, which have social, economic, political, and military repercussions in the international echo chamber of our modern world, should be sufficient to deter unilateral pacific blockade enthusiasts. In addition, a military response by the blockaded nation would certainly convince the enforcing state that such a flagrant violation of the rules could not be demurely accepted. Therefore, the only foreseeable results of this naval doctrine would be universal disgust, regional discredit, individual aggravation, and the unwarranted escalation of a problem which could have been better resolved by other methods.

Unilateral pacific blockade will, however, be brought forward for consideration again and again, for it is an attractive package to many Navy officers. When not opened carefully, however, it releases a Pandora's box of interpretations which sustain themselves wingless in flight by their sheer will to fly.

Newer concepts, which should have led to a better re-evaluation of blockades, were quite applicable during the Cuban quarantine; and, if they had been formidably projected, they might have enhanced United States arguments that a new legal norm for *regional* action (rather than unilateral) had been born.

Quarantine's validity under international law was refuted

by many experts merely because it was equated with the archaic concepts of maritime contraband. This tendency by many international lawyers to drive in reverse, usually toward the safe haven of unilateral pacific blockade, weakened the analytical foundation of what could have been positive arguments for collective quarantines under the U.N. Charter.

Simply stated, a collective quarantine might be considered to contain the following *proposed* elements:

1. effected by a regional agency, e.g., NATO,
2. implemented by *combined* naval forces,
3. submitted for Security Council approval (but *imposed* while awaiting decision),
4. based on reasonable necessity,
5. directed to use proportional measures,
6. controlled by a *regional* commander,
7. activated only within the region,
8. restricted to the high seas,
9. warranted for specific materials, and
10. confined to a definite area.

There are puddles of significant depth in these ten propositions, but at least an attempt can be made to wade through them toward a new doctrine. Otherwise panic again may follow surprise, for mob action can figuratively exist even within the staid and enlightened community of nations.

A Staff Should Be Shaped to Lean On

Illiterate leisure is a form of death—a living tomb.

Seneca

Most large ships have the misfortune to have an admiral's flag staff attached to them. This wartime umbilical necessity is, in time of peace, at best an inconvenience and at worst an administrative plague.

First, the staff has to be handled tenderly (because of its seniority). Second, it has to be catered to, for staff officers need the ship's enlisted personnel to take care of their laundry, food, and technical demands (the admiral's TV, the admiral's barge, the admiral's car radio). Third, staffs also require shipboard support, such as printing, weather, electronic, photographic, logistic, intelligence and communication services from the ship's officers and men. These requirements double the normal demands on shipboard personnel.

Despite the negative aspects of this inevitable staff transplant, the situation at least remained tenable and the association bearable (though not affectionate) until recent years. Ships just cannot afford these afloat staffs today because of the constant and inordinate decrease in the number of assigned personnel on fleet ships.

The staffs, though recognizing the shipboard personnel problems, find themselves both powerless to pursue a solution on behalf of the ships and disinclined to alleviate the situation by disembarking to a shipyard sanctuary.

To be perfectly frank, the need for so many staffs on so many ships in the light of modern and rapid communications and diminished manpower is minimal. Even this logic could be suppressed, however, if it could be determined that the staffs somehow

69

contributed to the efficiency of operations or the welfare of individual units. Instead, they lead a peacetime life of illiterate leisure, a tedium broken only occasionally by the intense, undirected efforts of some misassigned staff officer who sincerely wants to do something positive. This rare and sincere individual finds staff duty boring and usually ends up writing directives which require additional reports from the overworked ship's operating forces. These reports, of course, are either redundant, irrelevant, or inane. Therefore, the only recourse a wise commanding officer has when dynamic staff officers are attached to the flag unit on his ship is to direct staff officer energies toward some project that will least interfere with operations—such as a ping pong tournament.

Additionally, the flag officer's staff is usually accomodated on the largest ship in the force—for the staff's convenience! Instead, staff officers should rotate among their ships, living with the units having the weakest structures. In this way the staff could at least attempt to assist, to strengthen and to build the entire force into a better and more coordinate group. A staff's value to the most senior ship is sometimes questionable—and often unjustifiable when compared with the needs of smaller elements in the force.

Commanding officers of the smaller ships, conversely, often have to spend a great deal of their time trekking over to the larger ship, hat in hand and begging pardon, to explain why they can't perform as well as the staff's directives say they must. The fact that they do not have the number of personnel they require nor the number of technicians they need nor the number of mature enlisted petty officers they were promised, nor the school quotas they asked for nor the shore based support they deserve nor the installation and repair funds they were planning on is, from the staff viewpoint, a poor excuse for not supporting the flag unit.

For over seven years (since 1965) the poor bloodied commanding officers of Navy ships have been doing so much with so little for so long that now they are expected to do everything with nothing. This is the "can do" spirit which staffs expect and demand, and it is further reflected in the nit-picking remarks directed at individual units not only by staffs, but also by fleet refresher training groups (check-mates), operational readiness inspection teams, and every other critical desk dean who administers judgement from his nonoperational parochial perch. It is also the attitude which has, in part, driven down the officer retention and enlisted re-enlistment rates.

70

The number of hours which are required of shipboard operational personnel is approximately twice that of their civilian counterparts. To do this labor for poor pay under strict discipline is requesting a lot; but to also criticize the effort strains individual sensibilities and ignores common sense. In today's relatively affluent civilian society the trained officer or petty officer just doesn't have to subject himself to such a carping environment. And, after his required tour of duty is up, today's skilled Navy man too often heads for greener and more pleasant pastures.

Staffs could also help alleviate many problems not only by often basing themselves ashore (for those which must exist), but also by permanently assigning their personnel to live among all the ships in the force for the purpose of aiding, rather than burdening, their individual units. They could also take a more considerate attitude toward the undermanned ships of the Navy, and fight harder to assure that they are manned properly in the future. There is a reason, a purpose, and a benefit in having some (fewer) flag staffs. But it is time to re-analyze and determine staff values in order to eliminate the subsidiary and parasitic elements which have evolved. A good place to start is for each staff to ask itself, "What good am I to my units?" Other questions will follow in surprising sequence.

The Lamb Chops Is On Thursday

I don't s'pose there's anybody on this earth likes gingerbread as well as I do; and I don't s'pose there's anybody gets less of it.

A. Lincoln

The continuing controversy over military commissaries has probably misled millions of Americans into believing that the armed forces are stuffing themselves with ten cent chops and two bit steaks at the taxpayer's expense. On behalf of those harried military wives who plow the tin canned furrows of every over-crowded commissary aisle throughout the world, the myth must be destroyed.

The only reason that military wives even paw through wilted lettuce is that each purchase saves a few pennies which, in aggregate, total a munificent sum of five or ten dollars a week per family. The amount (and the food) need be neither challenged nor envied.

In actual fact, the price differential between civilian super-markets and commissaries is very small. In many instances, such as fresh fruit, vegetable produce, and meats, the civilian markets can undercut the commissaries through chain purchases and better management techniques (Amen!).

Additionally, there is no consistency in prices from base to base, and military families often pay one-third higher prices at one station than they do at another. For example, milk was ten to fifteen cents higher per half gallon at one major East Coast base than at its West Coast counterpart in the same month. (What ever happened to the fable of "slightly higher West of the Mississippi?)

Of course Mrs. Navy Seaman need not shop at the commissaries; but five or ten dollars a week is more important to her and her military family than it is to the family of her civilian neighbor.

Her husband, you see, only makes about eighty dollars a week; and if he gets promoted all the way up to second class petty officer (or Marine sergeant) after four years of service, he will make over one hundred dollars a week. (If he is a military electronics technician or airplane mechanic, this is less than half of the basic key amount paid to his civilian colleague.)

As expected, the thrifty military spouse therefore "comparison shops" at the commissary for some foodstuffs and at the local markets for others (especially weekday bargains). This rag-picking existence takes a considerable amount of time, but it does save a modicum of money.

Rather than snipe at commissaries, then, there should be more attention given as to why they are necessary and how they could be improved.

First, they exist because they are a less expensive way to compensate for actual wages than paying military personnel equivalent civilian salaries. Also, it is a cheap way to allege that the enlisted man has monumental hidden benefits from his secret grocery store—a fable of goodness and goodies, if believed, where there exists a veritable horn of plenty which the military jealously guards from the prying eyes of their less fortunate civilian friends. That theory is annually propounded by economic idiots. It prevents military pay raises and, coincidentally, does nothing to retain servicemen. Pry away! Shop! (Military wives will be glad to counsel the ignorant.) Most especially, visit the more remote bases— say, like somewhere more than twenty miles from the Pentagon. And don't expect a wide display of meat. Remember, "the lamb chops is on Thursday."

Second, commissaries can't be improved until they are expanded beyond the limits of their World War II walls (which hold up the leaking roofs of temporary buildings built for expediency thirty years ago). The commissaries also need experienced, long term, particularly trained, and reasonably dedicated management teams (although, to give due credit, the officers and men running commissaries do their best with what they have—which isn't much).

Incidentally, the uninitiated should also visit the homes where the families of the enlisted men live to appreciate why seemingly trivial commissary savings are really important. At many bases the military man has only two choices—either to be gouged by landlords or to locate his family far from the base.

Since, in the Navy, he often serves his nation away from home, he enjoys his family's occasional presence with more than routine affection. But he enjoys it at unbearable expense.

One enlisted man with over ten years service (a first class petty officer) stated that "the only people living in the civilian housing area with me are other enlisted families and welfare recipients."

But what of base housing for enlisted men? Oh! Well, for a brief moment in 1964, some military leaders actually took base housing seriously!

The Mark of Zorro!

The only mistake the Navy made in the Pueblo Case was in not selling the ship to the Israelis on an as is—where is basis.

Anonymous

Since the arrival of Admiral Zumwalt in the Pentagon as the new Chief of Naval Operations (CNO) there have been only two prime degrees of administrative effort—CNO "Urgent" correspondence, and other items.

Unlike the more apostolic cerebrations which flutter down as omniscient directives from the Joint Chiefs of Staff (JCS), the new CNO guidelines attempt to involve the Navy in the "now world." For example, his hot ship (active vessel) transfers of older ships to other nations, his overseas involvement plans for Navy men and their families, and his close ties with naval leaders from most nations have effected an international liberalization of maritime policies which are, for the most staid of military departments, radical departures from the Navy's historical conservatism.

Of course, CNO still has many discomfiting problems, many of which are inherent. The organization he inherited is too huge to manage. Additionally, the CNO is surrounded with a super staff of horse holders (or line handlers) who often think up ideas for others to investigate. This breeds a particular discontent down at the action officers' level based on the premise that "he who complains about the food should assist in the kitchen." Whether the novel ideas generated are good or bad, it is felt that the CNO courtier who has a mystical vision should saddle up his own question and help the action officers brand stray answers.

In addition to the internal woes of the continuing "ivy tower concept," the CNO has a personal staff which has about as many officers as the entire State Department. The product of such a behemoth is the staff answer—which is a general proposition and which is seldom worth a damn. If it is true, according to the Peter

Principle, that "...the damage caused by unnecessary people is about equal to the square of their number," then CNO possesses a potential disaster area.

Another facet of the bureaucratic lather and lava which flows toward CNO is that an action officer's proposal to CNO can be engulfed in administrative goop by senior officers who either do not like or do not agree with innovative ideas. This leads to an organizational maze whereby the majority of younger OpNav officers, who agree with CNO's modern policies, occasionally have their energies and efforts redirected by those few senior OpNav officers who may not agree with the new CNO.

And if action officers become overly enthusiastic about CNO's goals or game plans when their seniors are lukewarm, some personal parapets appear. (Careers can be mutilated at the lower level of bureaucracy if one fails to learn that an ounce of loyalty is sometimes worth a pound of brains.)

A typical CNO works about 72 hours a week at the Pentagon, attends daily ceremonies and parties, and takes home two suitcases of work every night. He needs a chief saint as an aide and archangels for his staff. Unfortunately, most senior OpNav officers are more biased than blessed. They are, in the classic sense, prima donnas, since their fine operational records, advanced academic degrees, and proven leadership abilities were the very qualities they acquired in the 26 to 30 years of service that contributed to their selection as counselors at the citadel.

But such expertise compounds every problem. Each program under review receives such a knowledgeable "wash" before any proposals reach CNO that the results often are bleached and mangled until they are devoid of color or shape. Thus CNO receives the infamous staff answer, brought to him in living grey. The process is diverting, but destructive; in essence, an instant administrative beatification with concurrent beheading. This Pentagon procedure always blesses the soul of each proposal just as the officious guillotine drops, assuring that the brain will not activate.

Of course, proper staffing also requires that an action officer should receive some guidance or direction when tasked to accomplish a mission. But not in the Pentagon. Instead, he receives only a mandate in memo form that usually allows minimum time for response. With his short due date in mind and his memo in hand, the action officer then takes off, often in a tangential direction, in a vain attempt to locate the author of the unique problem that he is now charged to investigate. This is because in true staff fashion he usually is not provided with either the name of the originator or guidance by seniors who have casually initialed the memorandum as it descended. He also is not privy to what CNO or other flag officers thought of the idea as it meandered earthward into his hands. And, since the action officer has no way of knowing what the originator had in mind when his cerebral corn popped, he really has no insight into the decision that sent the particular item to him in the first place. However, since action officers are imbued with Navy spirit, unquestioning allegiance, and dogmatic determination, they research, query, outline, and answer each memo in true staff fashion, heavenward through the chain of command. Their implementation plans, then, become the basis for a new CNO program. Is this correct? Not very damn likely!

This is now the time that all the senior officers who had no contributory thoughts on the down slope become avid ski enthusiasts as the program is towed toward the mountain peak—CNO's office. The action officer who could not, as we have mentioned, get anyone to help with the plowing, now finds that his harvest grain is examined microscopically for administrative fungus.

Since the Pentagon was designed so that senior officers could take sides on any issue and still have one left over, any program proposal going toward CNO usually is bounced back to the action officer time and again until the final answer is bland enough for everyone to stomach. As served, it seldom resembles the dish originally concocted. The point is that in removing the flavor, CNO sometimes receives neither the action officer's recipe, nor anything substantive that he can digest. If no action can be subsequently directed because the proposed program, as approved, appears exceptionally weak, then everyone can sit back contentedly until the next rocket is launched. Since the CNO staff has long chains in many directions, no single person in any one chain of command can ever be charged with killing a particular program; yet many good ideas are smothered. This method of administrative death by disassociation always is effective—and it leaves the staff survivors blameless.

What any CNO needs is a compact staff to provide immediate answers in a more direct manner. But in the Washington heirarchy, every attempt at change produces only a momentary illusion. In OpNav, and in other military staffs as well, a scimitar would be required to slice the uncultivated administrative nut in order to reach organizational meat. Even then it is quite likely that the post-World War II husk would resist surgery. Entrenched positions are never easy to attack in combat; in a bureaucracy they are near-impregnable.

Composed in CRT Times Roman by the George Banta Company, Menasha, Wisconsin.

Printed and bound on the Cameron Belt Press by the Kingsport Press, Kingsport, Tennessee.

Jacket/Cover illustration by Robert Osborn.